Bishop's

The Cookbook

Bishop's

The Cookbook

John Bishop

with additional recipes by

Michael Allemeier, Dennis Green and Tina Perenseff

Douglas & McIntyre

VANCOUVER / TORONTO

Douglas & McIntyre Ltd.
1615 Venables Street
Vancouver, British Columbia V5L 2H1

Canadian Cataloguing in Publication Data
Bishop, John, 1944-
Bishop's

ISBN 1-55054-437-3

1. Cookery—British Columbia—Vancouver. 2. Bishop's (Restaurant) I.
Title.
TX945.5.B5B57 1996   641.59711'33   C95-911221-9

Editing by Saeko Usukawa
Design by George Vaitkunas
Photographs by John Sherlock
Editorial Assistance by Elizabeth Wilson and Naomi Pauls
Printed and bound in Canada by Friesens
Printed on acid-free paper

The publisher gratefully acknowledges the assistance of the Canada Council
and of the British Columbia Ministry of Tourism, Small Business and Culture.

Bishop's would like to thank Stephen Wong of Mōt'iv for the dinnerware used
in the colour photographs.

In Appreciation

*My warmest thanks to all the Bishop's customers new and old, to the
loyal, hard-working staff led by restaurant manager and sommelier Abel Jacinto,
and to sous-chef Dennis Green. I am especially grateful to my chef
and friend Michael Allemeier, without whom this collection of recipes
could not have been put together.*

*I also thank Mr. Peter Barry of Kinsale, who gave me responsibility and example,
and whose influence on me continues to this day; David Robinson
and Zonda Nellis, who named the restaurant and helped guide me through my
first art acquisitions; my brother, Adrian, who spread the word about Bishop's
throughout his travels; my friend and dentist Bud Sipko for his support,
and my artist friends for allowing me into their lives.
Robert Simpson of Liberty Wines helped me with the wine suggestions.*

*I would like to dedicate this book to my family, friends, customers and staff—
and to my mother, Irene, who first let me into the kitchen.*

Contents

To Jackie,
    Best Wishes + Bon appetit!
        John Burton Race oct 96.

An introduction to Bishop's Restaurant

by John Bishop

I'M CONSTANTLY AMAZED by the people who turn up at my restaurant. When we pick up the phone, we never know who's coming—movie star, prime minister, prince, artist, tycoon, author, diva. However, the biggest compliment we get is not from the celebrities or the guidebooks or the restaurant reviews, but from customers who come to dine time after time. We consider them as family.

It's odd that Bishop's turned out the way it did.

When chefs get together on their days off, they love to have dinner parties for all their friends and talk about what their restaurant will be like when they open it. At my dinner parties, we used to talk about how you can't go to a restaurant and do just what we were doing—sit around a table and get a whole chicken served family-style. I thought it would be neat to have a restaurant like that.

Then, when I was ready to go out on my own, I took a trip to New York and went to a restaurant that astonished me. They used beautiful china and Christofle silver and the best crystal, but there was modern art dripping off the walls and big flower arrangements. Here were all the trappings of a wonderful French restaurant, but no stuffiness. And, oh my God, the food! It was classic French cooking, but absolutely modern, with locally grown ingredients presented in a wonderful array of colours and shapes and all tasting very natural. In every way, this restaurant had a classical feel to it, but it was also very contemporary.

So, out went the family-style idea. This approach felt so right that I was absolutely driven. I'd found what I wanted to create. It wasn't a great time to open a restaurant then—it was 1985 and the recession was still on—but none of my friends were surprised when they found out what I was about to do.

I'll never forget that first day. An hour before the doors opened, the furniture was still being moved; Theresa, my wife, was hanging the blinds she had made; my lawyer, Rick, was wallpapering the bathroom; soups and stocks were simmering on the stove. At the last minute, we realized we didn't know what to do with the napkins, so we arranged them in the wineglasses—a desperate move that became something of a signature of the restaurant. A week before, a friend had passed by and thought we'd never make it; he wondered if he should cancel the flowers he'd arranged to send. But he kept the faith, and, miraculously, we did pull things together and had a great opening party.

At first, I cooked and at the same time attempted to greet my customers as they arrived, because I was the only one who knew the guests well. But after six months I was forced to change roles, put on a suit and try to cover the front of the house while also exerting some influence on the food. That's the way I still operate.

We want to present perfect, understated, delicious food with everything thought out. I'd call our style of cuisine international new food. We have a very creative style of cooking that's grounded in a European tradition. The cooking methods are still roasting, grilling, poaching and steaming—and our preparation techniques are still classic. We're not reinventing the wheel, but we do stay away from the fussy and the ridiculously complicated. Who needs it when you have flavourful fresh ingredients to start with?

Ingredients are king—we look for quality and freshness. It's sort of a Japanese attitude: if you buy a fish that's just out of the ocean, you don't need to do a lot to it. And we don't apply the principle just to the centrepiece ingredient. The vegetables are local and organic, bright and delicious. The breads are baked every morning.

We play with food the same way an artist plays with paints. We let the ingredients tell us what to cook. A supplier brings in a load of razor clams, and they become our evening special. Someone picks a bunch of elderberry blossoms from a tree growing wild, and their distinctive fragrance inspires a sauce. Blackberries come into season, and we consider the possibilities of using them different ways, perhaps in a meat dish. That's the fun of running a small restaurant.

We like to tinker. The innovation comes in combining flavours, textures, ethnic influences and colours, all with pleasure in mind. The vegetables might arrive as different vividly coloured purées, all shaken together to make abstract art on the plate. Or the mashed potatoes might be

sprinkled with a bit of coarse salt, so that with every forkful you get wonderful, unexpected high notes of salt. China might meet Mexico in a shellfish spring roll with a chipotle tomato sauce; a white fish fillet might look dramatic in a pool of red sauce.

People often look at the dishes we bring out and say, "I don't know whether to eat it or lacquer it and put it on the wall," but eat it they do, and they usually tell us that they're glad they did. We also hear, "I could do this at home," in a tone of some surprise. Absolutely! That's the whole point.

Chef Michael Allemeier presides in the kitchen now, cooking from the heart as he has for ten years. His cooking skills are world class, and he's also totally aware of issues surrounding food and food service. Those attributes make him an excellent teacher. Sous-chef Dennis Green also cooks like an angel, although his style differs slightly. He's brilliant with seafood dishes and creative desserts. Their two styles complement each other, and Dennis and Michael work together very well.

We also have a wonderful team of support people in the kitchen. Carolyn Wallace starts work every weekday morning at 6:30 to bake our breads and pastries and to prepare the soups and sauces. What a great cook she has become. Then there is David Kerry, who works closely with both chefs, and Charlene Henke and Claire May, who prepare the salads, appetizers and desserts.

In putting this book together, I wanted to keep the recipes simple. Yes, they're really interesting and involve lots of wonderful ingredients, but they're also easy to make. In fact, when we had our initial meetings about the book, we talked about how combinations of a few simple things are every bit as impressive as one complicated thing. For instance, serve homemade ice cream (which is not hard to make) with some of your own sugar cookies or gingersnaps. Serve a spaetzle that's flavoured to go with the main dish, and suddenly the dish is elevated. Mash the potatoes with roasted garlic, and change the everyday to the exotic.

We encourage you to make stocks and sauces for the freezer so they're there when you need them. These are the basics that we use to intensify flavours in dishes, and they aren't difficult to make. Having them on hand will improve your cooking immeasurably.

Over the years, we've developed close relationships with our suppliers because we depend so much on fresh, top-quality ingredients. Hazelmere Organic Farm even consults with us on which vegetables and herbs to plant. Unless you're a gardener yourself, you can't have that kind of control, but you can get to know the grocers and butchers and fishmongers that you normally deal with. Good customers get good service.

One of the things I used to love when I was cooking at home was the hours and hours of preparation. I'd put on some jazz, pour some wine, gather the ingredients and just spend hours putting a meal together. I don't have as much time now, so I tend to shop at the last minute and find something absolutely knockout that can be prepared in a very simple way. Many of these recipes are like that. Others may require more preparation, but they're still straightforward.

Of the hundreds of recipes we've prepared over the past ten years, we chose these because they are or were so popular with our customers. We've put in many suggestions for substitutions or variations, because that's how we like to work in our kitchen. In cooking, nothing remains the same. That to us is the tremendous fun of it. We hope that you will use and enjoy this book as an inspiration for your own creativity.

On wine and food

by John Bishop

I BEGAN LEARNING ABOUT WINE in the early 1960s when I lived and worked in Ireland. Ireland has a tremendous history in the wine trade, and many Irish families have historical links to the great French château families. Running the Man Friday restaurant in Kinsale was a wonderful experience. Local fish and game made up the menu, and our wine offerings were amazingly wide-ranging.

German white wines, with their lovely soft floral flavours, were very popular at the time, and perfect with our wonderful Dublin Bay prawns. The Irish are great meat-eaters, so for reds we served mostly wines from Burgundy and Beaujolais, with their earthy, mushroom, damp-cellar smells. And my wine education went on from there.

The Bishop's cellar is ten years old. We began, like most small restaurants, with a very humble budget. The wines were purchased almost daily, depending on how busy we were and how many bottles we'd sold the night before. If I remember correctly, we had ten reds and ten whites on the menu, all from either Europe or America. A lot has changed in ten years.

Every month's end, Abel Jacinto, our wine keeper and sommelier, spends two days checking and counting the stock. He, more than anybody, knows his way around the two cellars we now have. Wines for long-term keeping are stored at the bottom of piles of cases. Old Bordeaux are stored on their sides on racks. Everyday bottles of wine are kept in their original cases. Small amounts of premium wines are stored in bins. We change our wine list almost weekly, partly in order to offer more of our 3,000-bottle inventory and partly because we must constantly de-list the wines that sell out and list the new ones that come along.

When I think of wine, I nearly always think of food. That is not to say that wines cannot be enjoyed by themselves, but wines really do make a meal complete. Wine can bring together all the flavours if it is properly paired with food. There are many opinions on how to do this, and everyone's palate is different, but here are some ideas I've found successful.

In matching wine and food, the ideal is to create a balance so the flavours of both wine and food are allowed to come through and complement each other. There are a few ways to do this. You can choose wines that match the flavours and weight of the food—for instance, have a seasoned steak with a Rhône red to match the peppery qualities of both. Or match a fish dish that has a rich, creamy sauce with a sumptuous, oaky Chardonnay or Sémillon.

You can also choose wines that are a contrast to the dish and act as a palate cleanser—poached salmon is rich in flavour and oils, so a light but flavourful wine with good acid levels such as a Pinot Gris, Pinot Blanc or Sancerre will cut the richness and still stand up to the flavour. But for salmon that is grilled or barbecued—a style of cooking that creates more intense flavours—it is best to choose a bigger wine such as a Chardonnay, a rosé, or even a light red wine such as a Pinot Noir.

The combination of some dishes and wines adds an extra flavour element. When a heavy meat or game dish meets a hearty red wine such as a rich California Zinfandel or Cabernet, the complexities of both are heightened.

The clearest and most simple guideline is for dessert wines. The dessert should not be sweeter than the wine.

The serving temperature of a wine is a personal choice. Certain rich, full-flavoured white wines can be served at about 45°F (7°C). Lighter, possibly more acidic wines can be kept on ice throughout the meal. Champagnes and sparkling wines are always served chilled. A mature Cabernet and other similarly weighty wines I like to serve just below room temperature. Younger robust red wines can be served even a little cooler—55°F (13°C), which is an ideal cellar temperature. I enjoy pouring Pinot Noirs and some other red wines on the cool side and allowing them to evolve in the wineglass.

A proper wineglass enhances the flavour of the wine by concentrating the flavour and bouquet. The restaurant standard is Riedel crystal, which is available at select wine stores and by mail order. It is fragile and expensive, but also the best. For everyday use or for parties, I suggest going to a restaurant supply store and buying a case of thirty-six Stoddart 1003 glasses. These are reasonably priced, extremely durable and usually dishwasher safe.

Storing your wines is very important if you plan to keep them for a long time. If your home has a cool storage area where the temperature doesn't vary much from 55°C (13°C) and there's no vibration, that's good. Otherwise, you'll probably want to invest in a temperature-controlled storage unit, of which there are many types and sizes available. The key is maintenance, because if the cooling mechanism breaks down and the temperature rises, older, more fragile wines can suffer permanent damage.

Before you invest in a large amount of any wine, it is a good idea to purchase a sample bottle to taste or seek advice from your wine retailer or local wine columnist. Wine clubs offer different kinds of events at which you can taste and compare. Just remember that in spite of all the advice and of all the best suggestions and recommendations in the world, you should explore, discover and buy wines that you personally enjoy.

Throughout this book, I've suggested wines to accompany the dishes. I don't get too exact, as wines differ from label to label, and from vintage to vintage—but I do give an idea of the type of wine that will complement the flavours of the dish. The reward of matching wine and food is that when everything comes together, you produce a wonderful, harmonious, balanced, flavourful treat.

Oyster mushroom with rosemary soup

Carrot, coconut and ginger soup

Red pepper and celeriac corn chowder

Prawn bisque

Roasted eggplant, shiitake and pancetta soup

Halibut consommé

West Coast chowder

Oyster mushroom with rosemary soup

::

The rosemary brings out the woodsy flavour of the mushrooms. This recipe also works with shiitake or wild mushrooms.

SERVES 8

¼ cup	butter	60 mL
3	onions, sliced	3
2	garlic cloves, minced	2
5 sprigs	fresh rosemary	5 sprigs
½ cup	white wine	125 mL
2 lbs.	oyster mushrooms, chopped	1 kg
2 lbs.	field mushrooms, chopped	1 kg
8 cups	chicken stock (page 146)	2 L
4 cups	whipping cream	1 L
pinch	salt and pepper	pinch
	balsamic vinegar	

In a large soup pot, melt the butter, then sweat the onions, garlic and rosemary until fragrant.

Deglaze the pot with the white wine. Add the mushrooms, chicken stock and whipping cream.

Bring to a boil and simmer for 1 hour. Pass through a food mill and season.

Serve with some balsamic vinegar on the side—a few drops in the soup will bring out the flavours.

Carrot, coconut and ginger soup

::

You can taste the influence of Asia in the coconut milk, which is readily available in cans. Instead of carrots, you can use yams.

SERVES 8

¼ cup	butter	60 mL
3	onions, sliced	3
2	garlic cloves, minced	2
⅓ cup	ginger, peeled and grated	75 mL
½ cup	white wine	125 mL
12	carrots, chopped	12
4 cups	chicken stock (page 146)	1 L
4 cups	whipping cream	1 L
6 cups	coconut milk	1.5 L
pinch	salt and pepper	pinch

In a large soup pot, melt the butter, then sweat the onions, garlic and ginger until fragrant.

Deglaze the pot with the white wine. Add the carrots, chicken stock, whipping cream and coconut milk.

Bring to a boil and simmer for 1 hour. Pass through a food mill and season.

Red pepper and celeriac corn chowder

::

A lovely light soup—almost a broth, but with the texture of the corn.
Look for firm young celeriac (or celery root), as the older ones become woody and hollow in the middle.
Celeriac should still have the stems attached and should be green.

SERVES 8

4 ½ lbs.	red peppers	2 kg
	vegetable oil	
¼ cup	butter	60 mL
3	onions, sliced	3
2	garlic cloves, minced	2
I cup	celeriac, peeled and chopped	250 mL
I cup	white wine	250 mL
12 cups	chicken stock (page 146)	3 L
pinch	salt and pepper	pinch
2 cups	fresh corn kernels	500 mL

Preheat the oven to 450°F (230°C).

Rub the red peppers with a little vegetable oil and place in a pan. Roast in the oven for 8 to 10 minutes, turning occasionally, until the skin lifts. Reserve the juice.

Place the peppers in a bowl and cover tightly with plastic wrap. Let cool for 30 minutes, as this will make it easier to remove the skin. Cut each pepper in half, peel off the skin, then remove the core and seeds.

In a large soup pot, melt the butter, then sweat the onions, garlic and celeriac until tender.

Deglaze the pot with the white wine. Add the peppers, roasting juice and chicken stock. Bring to a boil and simmer for 1 hour.

Pass through a food mill and season. Add the corn and simmer for 5 minutes.

Prawn bisque

::

*Our customers love this velvety soup.
We have used crab or lobster for this recipe, but we keep
coming back to prawns because they're a little unusual.*

*To make Smoked Salmon Bisque, add 8 oz. (250 g) of
sliced smoked salmon after deglazing with the brandy
and leave out the prawns.*

SERVES 8

¼ cup	butter	60 mL
3	onions, sliced	3
½	garlic clove, minced	½
2	carrots, chopped	2
3 oz.	brandy	90 mL
4 cups	shellfish stock (page 147)	1 L
4 cups	tomato sauce (page 150)	1 L
2 cups	whipping cream	500 mL
pinch	salt and pepper	pinch
8 oz.	prawns	250 g

In a large soup pot, melt the butter, then sweat the onions, garlic and carrots until tender.

Deglaze the pot with the brandy. Add the shellfish stock, tomato sauce and whipping cream.

Bring to a boil and simmer for 1 hour. Pass through a food mill and season.

Peel and devein the prawns. Add to the soup as a garnish when reheating to serve.

Roasted eggplant, shiitake and pancetta soup

::

*Like a classic potage, this is a rich and satisfying soup—
thick and textured. If possible, make it the day before
you serve it. That way, it will develop an extra dimen-
sion of flavour. (In fact, that advice goes for all soups.)*

SERVES 8

2 lbs.	eggplant	1 kg
	vegetable oil	
1 Tbsp.	butter	15 mL
3	onions, sliced	3
½	garlic clove, minced	½
8 oz.	pancetta, sliced	250 g
1 tsp.	cracked chilies	5 mL
½ cup	white wine	125 mL
1 lb.	shiitake mushrooms, chopped	500 g
1 lb.	field mushrooms, chopped	500 g
8 cups	chicken stock (page 146)	2 L
4 cups	whipping cream	1 L

Preheat the oven to 450°F (230°C).

Cut the eggplant lengthwise into slices ½ inch (1.2 cm) thick, then rub with a little vegetable oil. Place the eggplant in a pan and roast in the oven for 20 to 25 minutes, until brown. Reserve the juice.

In a large soup pot, melt the butter, then sweat the onions, garlic, pancetta and cracked chilies until tender.

Deglaze the pot with the white wine. Add the eggplant, roasting juice and mushrooms. Sweat for 2 to 3 minutes.

Add the chicken stock and whipping cream. Bring to a boil and simmer for 1 hour. Pass through a food mill.

Halibut consommé

::

Consommé does take time and effort, but it's worth the trouble.
Nothing beats the pleasure of eating a well-made consommé. How can something
so perfectly clear and smooth have such a divine flavour?
The sweetness of the vermouth and the sherry works wonderfully with the halibut.

SERVES 8

CONSOMMÉ STOCK

16 cups	fish stock (page 147)	4 L
4 sprigs	fresh tarragon	4 sprigs
2 sprigs	fresh thyme	2 sprigs
1 oz.	red vermouth	30 mL
2 oz.	sherry	60 mL
pinch	salt and pepper	pinch

To make the consommé stock, bring the fish stock almost to a boil in a large pot. Be careful not to let it boil or it will become cloudy. Add the tarragon and thyme, then lower the heat to a simmer. Reduce the stock by ⅓.

Add the red vermouth and sherry to the reduced stock, then season. Let cool, then refrigerate *overnight*.

CLARIFICATION

1 lb.	fresh halibut	500 g
1	onion	1
4	carrots	4
2	celery stalks	2
1	leek	1
4 sprigs	fresh parsley	4 sprigs
12	egg whites	12

To make the clarification, place all the ingredients, except for the egg whites, in a food processor and grind until very finely chopped. Keep cold.

Fold the egg whites into the minced ingredients, until everything is fully incorporated. Whisk the mixture into the cold consommé stock.

Bring the stock gently to a simmer while stirring occasionally. When it comes to a simmer, stop stirring. Simmer for 1 hour—do not boil or the stock will become cloudy. The clarification ingredients create a "raft," which attracts impurities and floats to the top.

Push the raft gently aside to make a small window. Ladle out the cleared soup. Be careful not break the raft, or the consommé may cloud again. Strain the cleared soup through a cheesecloth.

West Coast chowder

::

Chunky and aromatic, with hints of fennel, coriander and juniper, this soup is sure to cure any rainy-day blues.

For red chowder, use tomato sauce.
For white chowder, use whipping cream instead of the tomato sauce.

SERVES 8

I lb.	clams	500 g
I lb.	mussels	500 g
I cup	white wine	250 mL
2 Tbsp.	clarified butter	30 mL
½ cup	onion, diced	125 mL
½ cup	carrot, diced	125 mL
½ cup	celery, diced	125 mL
½ cup	potato, diced	125 mL
¼ cup	pepper, diced	60 mL
¼ cup	zucchini, diced	60 mL
I tsp.	ground fennel seeds	5 mL
I tsp.	ground coriander seeds	5 mL
I tsp.	ground juniper berries	5 mL
I tsp.	dried basil	5 mL
I tsp.	dried oregano	5 mL
6 cups	tomato sauce OR whipping cream	1.5 L
8 cups	fish stock (page I47) plus nectar	2 L
I2	oysters, chopped	I2
6 slices	bacon	6 slices

In a large pot, steam the clams and mussels in ½ cup (125 mL) of the white wine for 5 to 10 minutes, until they open. Let cool, then shuck the clams and mussels. Reserve the liquid (called nectar).

In a large soup pot, melt the clarified butter, then sweat all the vegetables and herbs.

Deglaze the pot with the remaining ½ cup (125 mL) of the white wine. Add the tomato sauce (or whipping cream), fish stock and nectar.

Bring to a boil and simmer for 45 minutes. Add the clams, mussels and oysters.

While the soup is simmering, chop the bacon and fry in a pan. Drain on paper towels. Before serving the soup, garnish with the bacon.

Mussel gazpacho soup

Potato and pesto soup

Spicy cherry soup

Pear and cambozola soup

Mussel gazpacho soup

::

Mussels have a sweet flavour that works well with the sweetness of peppers and tomatoes.
Like all shellfish, they require a lot of respect—
steam them just until they open and be careful not to overcook them.

SERVES 4

2 lbs.	mussels	1 kg
4 cups	fish stock (page 147) plus nectar	1 L
1	cucumber	1
6	tomatoes	6
¼ cup	cucumber, diced	60 mL
¼ cup	tomato, diced	60 mL
¼ cup	red and yellow pepper, diced	60 mL
¼ cup	zucchini, diced	60 mL
¼ cup	onion, diced	60 mL
¼ cup	fresh corn kernels	60 mL
1	garlic clove, minced	1
1 bunch	fresh cilantro, chopped	1 bunch
½ bunch	fresh parsley, chopped	½ bunch
6 sprigs	fresh tarragon, chopped	6 sprigs
1	lime	1
pinch	salt and pepper	pinch

In a large pot, steam the mussels in ½ cup (125 mL) of the fish stock for 5 to 10 minutes, until they open. Let cool, then shuck the mussels. Reserve the liquid (called nectar).

Purée the 1 cucumber and 6 tomatoes in a food processor, until smooth. Pass through a sieve to remove any seeds and skin.

Add the remaining fish stock and the nectar to the tomato purée. Add all the diced vegetables, corn, garlic, herbs and mussels.

Add the juice of 1 lime. Season and let sit overnight in the refrigerator.

Potato and pesto soup

::

*We've modernized vichyssoise here. For this recipe,
use a good starchy potato (such as russet or red Pontiac)
so the soup has a smooth, creamy texture.*

SERVES 8

¼ cup	clarified butter	60 mL
3	onions, sliced	3
½	garlic clove, minced	½
6	potatoes, peeled and chopped	6
1 cup	white wine	250 mL
4 cups	chicken stock (page 146)	1 L
8 cups	whipping cream	2 L
pinch	salt and pepper	pinch
1 cup	basil pesto (page 151)	250 mL

In a large soup pot, melt the clarified butter, then sweat
the onions, garlic and potatoes until tender.

Deglaze the pot with the white wine. Add the chicken
stock and whipping cream. Bring to a boil and simmer for
1 hour.

Pass through a food mill, season and let cool. Whisk in
the pesto and serve.

Spicy cherry soup

::

Serve this soup at the beginning of a summer meal.
Cherries and red currants ripen
just when the first basil is coming up.
Bubbly mineral water gives this soup its effervescence,
but if you're feeling really decadent,
you can use Champagne. Instead of the red wine,
you can use raspberry or strawberry juice.

SERVES 8

I lb.	Bing cherries, pitted	500 g
8 oz.	red currants	250 g
I cup	orange juice	250 mL
4 cups	red wine OR raspberry or	I L
	strawberry juice	
2 sticks	cinnamon	2 sticks
6	cloves	6
4	whole star anise	4
I tsp.	nutmeg	5 mL
I tsp.	ground allspice	5 mL
4 oz.	fresh basil	125 g
2 cups	carbonated mineral water	500 mL

In a large bowl, combine all the ingredients (except for the carbonated mineral water). Pass through a food mill and chill.

Just before serving, add the carbonated mineral water.

Pear and cambozola soup

::

This is an intriguing winter soup that features
the classic combination of pear and blue cheese.
Our favourite pear for this soup is the Bosc.

SERVES 8

¼ cup	clarified butter	60 mL
3	onions, sliced	3
2 Tbsp.	garlic, minced	30 mL
8	ripe pears, cored and sliced	8
I cup	white wine	250 mL
8 cups	chicken stock (page 146)	2 L
4 cups	whipping cream	I L
8 oz.	cambozola cheese	250 g

In a large soup pot, melt the clarified butter, then sweat the onions, garlic and pears until fragrant.

Deglaze the pot with the white wine. Add the chicken stock and whipping cream. Bring to a boil and simmer for 1 hour.

Crumble the cambozola and whisk it into the broth. Pass through a food mill. Chill and serve.

Asparagus and minted new potato salad with sun-dried tomato mayonnaise

Heart of romaine salad with roasted beet vinaigrette

Bread salad with crisp pancetta

Gazpacho salad with roasted tomato vinaigrette

Warm mushroom pancetta salad with sherry vinaigrette

Arugula and strawberry salad

Butter lettuce with creamy herb dressing and toasted pine nuts

Spinach, poached pear and Parmesan salad

Tomato and arugula pesto salad

Winter greens with sun-dried cherry and thyme vinaigrette

Asparagus and minted new potato salad
with sun-dried tomato mayonnaise

::

This dish brings back fond memories for Michael Allemeier of
visiting his grandmother in England. Whenever she served minted new potatoes,
the aroma of mint filled the whole house.

SERVES 4

SUN-DRIED TOMATO MAYONNAISE

1 Tbsp.	sun-dried tomato, finely chopped	15 mL
2 Tbsp.	white wine OR water	30 mL
1 cup	mayonnaise (page 151)	250 mL
1 Tbsp.	fresh mint, chopped	15 mL

To prepare the mayonnaise, place the sun-dried tomato in the white wine (or water) in a small bowl to soak, preferably overnight, until the tomato fills out.

In a food processor, purée all the ingredients together until well mixed. Refrigerate until needed.

ASPARAGUS

24 stalks	asparagus	24 stalks
¼ cup	olive oil	60 mL
2 Tbsp.	raspberry vinegar	30 mL
	salt and pepper	

To prepare the asparagus, bring a large pot of salted water to the boil. Add the asparagus and cook for 3 to 5 minutes until done (some people like it crunchy, others like it well cooked). Cool at once in a bowl filled with iced water.

To prepare the vinaigrette, whisk together the olive oil and raspberry vinegar. In a bowl, toss the asparagus with the vinaigrette. Season and let sit for 1 hour before serving.

MINTED NEW POTATO SALAD

2 cups	very small new potatoes	500 mL
3 Tbsp.	fresh mint, chopped	45 mL
2 tsp.	salt	10 mL
	spinach OR pea tops	

To prepare the potato salad, place the potatoes, mint and salt in a saucepan. Cover the potatoes with cold water. Bring to a boil and simmer for 15 to 20 minutes until done. Drain and let cool.

In a bowl, toss the potatoes with the sun-dried tomato mayonnaise.

To assemble, lightly cover the bottom of each plate with a springtime green such as spinach (or pea tops). Mound the potato salad on top of the greens, then arrange the asparagus on top.

Heart of romaine salad
with roasted beet vinaigrette

::

This works as either a starter salad or a salade digestif.
We served it to Boris Yeltsin and Bill Clinton when they held their summit meeting in Vancouver in 1993.
The salad looked beautiful presented on the White House china.

SERVES 4

ROASTED BEET VINAIGRETTE		
2	medium beets (7 oz./200 g), tops and roots removed	2
1 cup	canola oil	250 mL
⅔ cup	cassis vinegar	150 mL
1 cup	olive oil	250 mL
1 tsp.	salt	5 mL

Preheat the oven to 350°F (180°C).

Rub the beets with a little of the canola oil and place them in a pan. Roast in the oven for about 30 minutes, turning every 5 minutes, until completely tender (when a knife can go through without resistance). Let cool, then peel and dice.

Place the beets in a food processor and purée, then slowly add the cassis vinegar, until it is all incorporated. With the motor still running, slowly add the remaining canola oil and the olive oil. Add the salt. Pass the vinaigrette through a fine sieve to remove any lumps.

2 heads	romaine lettuce	2 heads

Remove the large outer leaves from the romaine and soak the heads in cold water to wash. Remove from the water and drain. Refrigerate until needed.

When ready to serve the salad, use only the tender centre leaves of the romaine. Keep the leaves whole. In a large bowl, toss the romaine leaves with the vinaigrette. Fan out the romaine on each plate, using about half a head of lettuce per serving.

Bread salad with crisp pancetta

::

Michael Allemeier worked for some time in a Tuscan restaurant, and the influence shows in this recipe.
The salad should be served warm and slightly crisp.
This is the perfect way to use those leftover baguettes from last night's dinner party.

SERVES 4

VINAIGRETTE

1 cup	olive oil	250 mL
1/3 cup	balsamic vinegar	80 mL

To make the vinaigrette, whisk together the oil and vinegar.

BREAD SALAD

	olive oil	
1 cup	red onions, diced	250 mL
1 tsp.	garlic, minced	5 mL
1/2 cup	sun-dried tomatoes, sliced	125 mL
3 cups	day-old bread, cubed	750 mL
2 Tbsp.	fresh basil, chopped	30 mL
2 Tbsp.	fresh cilantro, chopped	30 mL
	salt and pepper	
8 slices	pancetta	8 slices
4 cups	salad greens, washed and dried	1 L

Preheat the oven to 400°F (200°C).

In a frying pan, heat a small amount of olive oil. Sauté the onions and garlic until tender. Add the sun-dried tomatoes and ¼ cup (60 mL) of the vinaigrette.

In a large bowl, toss the onion mixture with the bread, basil and cilantro. The bread should be slightly moist, so you may need to add a bit more vinaigrette. Season.

Place the pancetta on a baking sheet lined with parchment paper and crisp in the oven for 5 to 10 minutes. Drain on paper towels.

Place the bread salad in an ovenproof dish and heat in the oven for 5 to 10 minutes, or until warmed through and lightly toasted.

In a large bowl, toss the salad greens with some of the remaining vinaigrette. Arrange the greens on plates so that the leaves form a cup in the centre of each plate. Fill each lettuce cup with bread salad and garnish with the pancetta.

Gazpacho salad with roasted tomato vinaigrette

::

This salad can be a meal in itself.
The recipe uses all the usual gazpacho ingredients, and the roasted onion, garlic and tomatoes in the vinaigrette
add depth and richness without taking away any of the refreshing qualities.

SERVES 4

ROASTED TOMATO VINAIGRETTE

6	tomatoes	6
3	garlic cloves, peeled	3
I	small red onion, peeled	I
½ cup	extra virgin olive oil	125 mL
¾ cup	red wine vinegar	180 mL
pinch	salt and pepper	pinch

Preheat the oven to 400°F (200°C).

To make the vinaigrette, coat the tomatoes, garlic cloves and red onion with 1 Tbsp. (15 mL) of the olive oil. Place them in a pan and roast in the oven for ½ hour.

Place in a food processor with the vinegar and purée. With the motor still running, slowly add the remaining olive oil. Season.

GAZPACHO SALAD

½ cup	red pepper, diced	125 mL
½ cup	yellow pepper, diced	125 mL
½ cup	cucumber, diced	125 mL
½ cup	tomato, diced	125 mL
¼ cup	red onion, diced	60 mL
I cup	white bread, diced	250 mL
I Tbsp.	fresh basil, chopped	15 mL
I head	radicchio, washed and drained	I head

Place all the salad ingredients, except for the radicchio, in a large bowl and toss with the vinaigrette.

The radicchio is for garnish. Peel off the leaves carefully. Arrange the radicchio on plates so that the leaves form the shape of a cup and mound the salad in each one.

Warm mushroom pancetta salad
with sherry vinaigrette

::

This hot and cold salad consists of crisp dressed greens garnished with
warmed mushrooms, shallots and pancetta. Imagine a grey day warmed by a fire, this salad
and perhaps a bowl of West Coast Chowder (page 20) . . .

SERVES 4

SHERRY VINAIGRETTE

½ cup	sherry vinegar	125 mL
1 Tbsp.	honey	15 mL
½ cup	canola oil	125 mL
1 cup	olive oil	250 mL
pinch	salt	pinch
pinch	freshly ground pepper	pinch

MUSHROOM PANCETTA SALAD

8 cups	assorted salad greens	2 L
1 Tbsp.	olive oil	15 mL
½ cup	shallots, thinly sliced	125 mL
2 oz.	pancetta, thinly sliced	50 g
4 oz.	oyster mushrooms	125 g
¼ cup	dry sherry	60 mL

To prepare the vinaigrette, whisk together the first four ingredients. Season.

Wash and drain the salad greens. Place in a bowl and toss with enough of the vinaigrette to coat lightly. Arrange the salad greens on plates.

In a frying pan, heat the olive oil and sauté the shallots and pancetta until golden. Add the mushrooms and sauté until tender.

Deglaze the pan with the sherry and remove from the heat.

Arrange the salad greens on plates. Place the mushroom mixture and any pan juices over the salad greens. Serve at once.

Arugula and strawberry salad

∷

*This salad celebrates spring by using the first things to come up in the garden.
The strawberry vinegar is worth making during the season, but you can substitute Japanese rice wine vinegar
or a mild white wine vinegar, perhaps flavoured with tarragon.*

SERVES 4

STRAWBERRY VINEGAR

15-20	strawberries (8 oz./250 g)	15-20
¾ cup	white wine vinegar	200 mL

To prepare the vinegar, wash the strawberries in cold water, remove the stems and drain on paper towels.

Place the strawberries in a sterilized glass bottle or jar. Cover with the vinegar and close the top.

Let sit in a dark, cool, dry place for 2 to 4 weeks. After that, leave the strawberries in the vinegar, or strain the vinegar into a sterilized container. Enjoy!

The strawberry vinegar will keep for up to a year stored in a dark, cool, dry place, although the flavour will weaken over time.

STRAWBERRY VINAIGRETTE

¼ cup	strawberry vinegar	50 mL
⅓ cup	olive oil	75 mL
⅓ cup	canola oil	75 mL
	salt and cracked black pepper	

To prepare the vinaigrette, whisk together the strawberry vinegar, olive and canola oils. Season.

ARUGULA AND STRAWBERRY SALAD

24-30	strawberries (12 oz./350 g)	24-30
36 sprigs	arugula	36 sprigs
⅓ cup	toasted almonds, sliced	75 mL

To prepare the salad, wash the strawberries in cold water, then remove the stems. Add the strawberries to the vinaigrette, then cover and marinate for 2 to 3 hours at room temperature.

Wash the arugula in cold water and drain. Refrigerate until needed.

To serve the salad, arrange the arugula into a round wreath on each plate, leaving the centre clear. Toss the strawberries in the marinade to mix the ingredients, then spoon them into the centre of the arugula.

Drizzle the arugula with the vinaigrette as needed. Sprinkle with the toasted almonds. When serving, offer black pepper in a pepper mill.

Butter lettuce with creamy herb dressing and toasted pine nuts

::

This is about as simple and classic as you can get. Adding anything else to this salad would ruin it. The buttermilk in the dressing adds creaminess with a hint of tartness.

SERVES 4

CREAMY HERB DRESSING

2	egg yolks	2
I tsp.	Dijon mustard	5 mL
2 cups	fresh basil, chopped	500 mL
¼ cup	white wine vinegar	60 mL
I cup	canola oil	250 mL
½ cup	buttermilk	125 mL

To make the dressing, place the egg yolks, mustard, basil and vinegar in a food processor and purée. With the motor still running, slowly add the canola oil. Add the buttermilk and mix in.

2 heads	butter lettuce	2 heads
¼ cup	toasted pine nuts	60 mL

Wash and drain the butter lettuce. In a large bowl, toss the lettuce with the dressing and toasted pine nuts.

To serve, arrange the lettuce leaves in the form of 4 heads of butter lettuce, each in a shallow bowl.

Spinach, poached pear and Parmesan salad

::

For this dish, buy a solid piece of Parmesan cheese so that you can make big curls with a vegetable peeler. The pears are poached in Gewürztraminer syrup, and the spicy wine accentuates the other flavours in the dish.

SERVES 4

ROASTED GARLIC DRESSING

2	garlic cloves, peeled	2
I cup	extra virgin olive oil	250 mL
½ cup	fresh parsley, chopped	125 g
I cup	white wine vinegar	250 mL
I cup	canola oil	250 mL
pinch	salt and pepper	pinch

Preheat the oven to 400°F (200°C).

To prepare the dressing, drizzle the garlic cloves with a little of the olive oil. Place the garlic in a pan and roast in the oven for about 20 minutes until tender.

Place the roasted garlic, parsley and vinegar in a food processor and purée. With the motor still running, slowly add the rest of the olive oil and the canola oil. Season.

I lb.	spinach, washed and drained	500 g
2	poached pears (page 130), sliced	2
¼ cup	Parmesan cheese curls	60 mL

In a large bowl, toss the spinach with the dressing.

On the serving plates, lay out the spinach leaves like the spokes of a wheel. Arrange slices of poached pear in the centre of each plate and top with curls of Parmesan cheese.

Tomato and arugula pesto salad

::

Wait until the tomatoes in the garden are perfectly ripe before you make this salad.
The parsley helps tame the arugula in the pesto, as it can be a bit too peppery.
The arugula pesto also tastes wonderful on fish.
Try serving it with the Roast Ling Cod with Garlic Mashed Potatoes (page 78).

SERVES 4

ARUGULA PESTO		
2 cups	arugula (3 ½ oz./100 g)	500 mL
I cup	fresh parsley (I ½ oz./40 g)	250 mL
⅓ cup	toasted pine nuts	75 mL
I	garlic clove, peeled	I
⅓ cup	Parmesan cheese, grated	30 g
½ tsp.	salt	2 mL
½ cup	olive oil	125 mL

Wash and drain the arugula.

To make the pesto, place the arugula and parsley in a food processor and purée. Add the toasted pine nuts, garlic, Parmesan and salt, then grind to a paste. With the motor still running, slowly add the olive oil. Refrigerate until needed.

36 sprigs	arugula	36 sprigs
4	tomatoes	4
½ cup	olive oil	125 mL
½ cup	toasted pine nuts	125 mL

Wash the arugula leaves in cold water, drain and refrigerate until needed.

To serve the salad, divide the arugula into 4 portions and fan the sprigs out over half of each plate. Slice the tomatoes and fan them out on the other half of the plates. Spread the pesto over the tomatoes. Drizzle the olive oil over the arugula and sprinkle with the toasted pine nuts.

Winter greens with sun-dried cherry and thyme vinaigrette

::

Over the past few years, mixed salad greens have appeared in grocery stores everywhere. In winter, the greens are assertive. Use a combination of any of the following: witloof, radicchio, curly endive, arugula, mizumi, kale, chicory and hardy lettuces. Don't be conservative with the dressing. The winter greens can stand up to it.

SERVES 4

CHERRY AND THYME VINAIGRETTE

½ cup	black currant vinegar	125 mL
¼ cup	sun-dried cherries, minced	60 mL
1½ tsp.	fresh thyme leaves	7 mL
½ cup	olive oil	125 mL
½ cup	canola oil	125 mL
pinch	salt and pepper	pinch

To make the vinaigrette, place the vinegar, sun-dried cherries and thyme in a food processor. Blend until smooth. With the motor still running, slowly add the olive and canola oils. Season.

1 lb.	mixed winter greens, washed and drained	500 g

In a large bowl, toss the greens with the vinaigrette. To serve, arrange the salad loosely on plates.

Fried smelt with green herb and wasabi tartar sauce

Steamed clams with ale, pear and leek

Grilled calamari with sesame soy tomato coulis

Cornmeal-crusted oysters with grainy mustard mousseline

Grilled Japanese eggplant with chili sesame vinaigrette

Corn and chanterelle bread pudding

Scallop and prawn spring rolls with chipotle tomato sauce

Fresh foie gras with pea tops and rhubarb compote

Chanterelle, goat cheese and pepper strudel

Fried smelt
with green herb and wasabi tartar sauce

::

Smelt are very small fish. The smaller ones can be eaten whole.
The larger ones are easy to fillet: use the backbone as a guide and leave the skin on.
At the restaurant, we serve this dish with shoestring potatoes.

SERVES 4

GREEN HERB AND WASABI TARTAR SAUCE		
½ cup	red onion, finely diced	125 mL
⅓ cup	cornichons, finely diced	80 mL
¼ cup	fresh chives, finely chopped	60 mL
½ cup	fresh parsley, chopped	125 mL
2 Tbsp.	capers, finely chopped	30 mL
I cup	mayonnaise (page 151)	250 mL
2 Tbsp.	wasabi powder	30 mL
3 Tbsp.	cold water	45 mL

¼ cup	vegetable oil	60 mL
½ cup	flour	125 mL
4-8	smelt	4-8
	salt and pepper	

To make the sauce, combine the red onion, cornichons, chives, parsley and capers in a bowl. Add the mayonnaise and mix well.

In another bowl, mix together the wasabi powder and cold water to make a paste. Stir the wasabi paste into the mayonnaise mixture. Refrigerate for 2 hours before serving.

Add the oil to a frying pan over medium heat.

Lightly flour the smelt. Carefully place the fish in the hot oil and cook 2 to 3 minutes per side. Drain on paper towels and season.

To serve, place a dollop of the green herb and wasabi tartar sauce on each plate, and arrange the smelt next to the sauce. Offer more sauce on the side.

Steamed clams
with ale, pear and leek

::

A great winter dish.
Try using an ale from a microbrewery, or, if you have
an ale that you like to drink, use that. The beer for this
dish can range from pale ale to dark ale, but not stout.

SERVES 4

1	red pepper	1
	vegetable oil	
2 lbs.	fresh clams in the shell	1 kg
1	pear, sliced	1
1 cup	ale	250 mL
½ cup	leek, julienne	125 mL

Preheat the oven to 450°F (230°C).

Rub the red pepper with a little vegetable oil and place in a pan. Roast in the oven for 8 to 10 minutes, turning occasionally, until the skin lifts. Reserve the roasting juice.

Place the pepper in a bowl, then cover tightly with plastic wrap. Let cool for 30 minutes, as this will make it easier to remove the skin. Cut the pepper in half, peel off the skin, then remove the core and seeds. Cut into slices ½ inch (1.2 cm) wide.

Place the clams in a large pot and add all the other ingredients. Cover and bring to a boil, then reduce the heat and simmer for 5 to 10 minutes, until all the clams open.

To serve, divide the clams into four bowls, then spoon the pear, leek, red pepper and liquid over them.

Grilled calamari
with sesame soy tomato coulis

::

For this dish, it's important to buy small calamari. Buy fresh ones if at all possible.
If you must buy frozen calamari, find ones that are frozen whole and clean them yourself,
as the already cleaned frozen product doesn't do justice to this dish.

SERVES 4

I	red pepper	I
	canola oil	

Preheat the oven to 450°F (230°C).

Rub the red pepper with a little canola oil and place in a pan. Roast in the oven for 8 to 10 minutes, turning occasionally, until the skin lifts.

Place the pepper in a bowl, then cover tightly with plastic wrap. Let cool for 30 minutes, as this will make it easier to remove the skin. Cut the pepper in half, peel off the skin, then remove the core and seeds. Slice thinly. Set aside until needed.

MARINADE		
I tsp.	garlic, chopped	5 mL
I tsp.	coriander seeds	5 mL
I Tbsp.	fresh parsley, chopped	15 mL
I tsp.	pink peppercorns, crushed	5 mL
½ tsp.	cracked chilies	2 mL
I tsp.	ginger powder	5 mL
¼ cup	canola oil	60 mL
I lb.	squid tubes, cleaned (reserve tentacles)	500 g

To make the marinade, combine all the ingredients (except for the squid) in a bowl. Place the squid tubes in this mixture and marinate for 2 to 3 hours in the refrigerator. Set the tentacles aside in the refrigerator and do not marinate them.

SESAME SOY TOMATO COULIS

2 cups	tomato sauce (page 150)	500 mL
¼ cup	heavy cream	60 mL
2 Tbsp.	soy sauce	30 mL
1 Tbsp.	sesame oil	15 mL
1 tsp.	cracked chilies	5 mL
1 tsp.	garlic powder	5 mL
1 tsp.	ginger powder	5 mL

To make the coulis, whisk together all the ingredients in a saucepan. Bring to a simmer over medium-low heat, stirring frequently. Simmer for 10 minutes, then strain and set aside.

¼ cup	leek, julienne	60 mL
1 tsp.	canola oil	5 mL

Drain the squid tubes and discard the marinade. Cook the squid tubes on a hot grill for about 1 minute per side, until slightly opaque and puffed out.

In a small frying pan, heat the canola oil and sauté the tentacles with the leek and roasted red pepper until tender.

GARNISH

1 Tbsp.	pink peppercorns, crushed	15 mL
1 Tbsp.	fresh parsley, chopped	15 mL
1 Tbsp.	toasted sesame seeds	15 mL
1 Tbsp.	citrus zest	15 mL

To serve, spread the coulis in a pool in the centre of each plate. Lay out the squid tubes like the spokes of a wheel, with the tips pointing out.

Fill the centre of each plate with the sautéed tentacles and vegetables. Garnish with a sprinkle of crushed pink peppercorns, chopped parsley and toasted sesame seeds. Top the centre with a little citrus zest.

Cornmeal-crusted oysters
with grainy mustard mousseline

::

This savoury mousseline is incredibly light.
Refrigerate it as soon as you've made it so that it won't collapse.

SERVES 4

GRAINY MUSTARD MOUSSELINE		
1 cup	whipping cream	250 mL
2½ Tbsp.	grainy Dijon mustard	40 mL
½ cup	mayonnaise (page 151)	125 mL
½ tsp.	salt	2 mL
2 tsp.	fresh chives, chopped	10 mL
2 tsp.	fresh parsley, chopped	10 mL

To prepare the mousseline, whip the whipping cream until stiff peaks form.

In a separate bowl, combine the mustard, mayonnaise, salt, chives and parsley.

Carefully fold the mayonnaise mixture into the whipped cream, just enough to combine all the ingredients. Refrigerate until needed.

12	large beach oysters, shucked	12
½ cup	milk	125 mL
1 cup	yellow cornmeal	250 mL
	vegetable oil for frying	

Place the shucked oysters in the milk and let sit for 5 minutes. Drain the oysters and roll them in the cornmeal until they are evenly covered.

Heat a large heavy frying pan over medium heat. Add the vegetable oil to a depth of ½ inch (1.2 cm). Once the oil is hot, carefully add the oysters and cook for 4 minutes per side or until done.

Drain the oysters on paper towels and serve at once. Place a dollop of the mousseline in the centre of each plate and arrange the oysters around it.

Grilled Japanese eggplant
with chili sesame vinaigrette

::

This light vegetarian dish can be a starter or a whole meal.
The long, skinny Japanese eggplants don't have to be salted like the larger Italian eggplants,
and the skin is very tender. If you wish, you can add other vegetables
suitable for grilling, including summer squash, mushrooms and firm roma tomatoes.

SERVES 4

CHILI SESAME VINAIGRETTE		
½ cup	rice vinegar	125 mL
2 Tbsp.	soy sauce	30 mL
½ tsp.	chili flakes	2 mL
½ tsp.	ginger, peeled and grated	2 mL
½ tsp.	garlic, minced	2 mL
1 cup	vegetable oil	250 mL
½ cup	sesame oil	125 mL
1 Tbsp.	fresh lime juice	15 mL

To prepare the vinaigrette, whisk together all the ingredients in a bowl.

1 lb.	Japanese eggplants	500 g
	salt and pepper	
1	red pepper, sliced into 8 wedges	1

Cut the eggplants lengthwise into slices ½ inch (1.2 cm) thick. Season and drizzle with just enough of the vinaigrette to moisten.

Grill the slices of eggplant and pepper for 2 to 3 minutes per side until tender. Arrange on plates and drizzle with some more of the vinaigrette.

Corn and chanterelle bread pudding

::

Finally, here's a use for day-old cornbread. Fresh cornbread would absorb too much liquid and lose its texture.

*If you can't find fresh chanterelles, try the canned ones, but don't use dried ones,
as they simply don't soften in water. Feel free to substitute shiitake or oyster mushrooms.*

For a light lunch, serve this with a salad or soup.

SERVES 4

1 Tbsp.	olive oil	15 mL
¼ cup	red onion, diced	60 mL
½ cup	chanterelles	125 mL
1 cup	milk	250 mL
1	egg yolk	1
1	egg	1
½ cup	fresh corn kernels	125 mL
2 Tbsp.	fresh cilantro, chopped	30 mL
½ tsp.	salt	2 mL
1½ cups	day-old cornbread (page 142)	375 mL
2 Tbsp.	melted butter	30 mL

Preheat the oven to 350°F (180°C).

In a frying pan, heat the olive oil and sauté the red onion until tender. Add the chanterelles and sauté for 3 minutes over medium heat, then let cool.

In a saucepan, heat the milk to just under a simmer. Whisking all the time, slowly add the milk to the egg yolk and egg in a bowl.

Add the chanterelle mixture, corn, cilantro and salt to the milk. Crumble the cornbread into the mixture and combine well.

Brush four ramekins generously with the melted butter. Pour the pudding mixture into the buttered ramekins.

Place the ramekins in a roasting pan, then fill the pan almost up to the top with boiling water. Place this bain-marie in the oven and bake for 25 to 30 minutes until done. Remove from the oven and let the ramekins cool in the water.

Serve the pudding either still in the ramekins or unmould onto individual plates.

Scallop and prawn spring rolls
with chipotle tomato sauce

::

A chipotle is a dried, smoked jalapeño pepper. Spring roll wrappers are available fresh at most Asian food stores.
Make the sauce first, as once you've assembled the spring rolls,
you should cook them within half an hour, otherwise the wrappers might break.
The seafood inside quickly steams as the outside becomes crisp.

SERVES 4

CHIPOTLE TOMATO SAUCE

12	tomatoes	12
2 Tbsp.	canola oil	30 mL
I	onion, sliced	I
4	garlic cloves, minced	4
2	chipotles, finely chopped	2
½ cup	red wine	125 mL
½ cup	tomato sauce (page 150)	125 mL

SPRING ROLLS

8 oz.	scallops, chopped	250 g
8 oz.	prawns, chopped	250 g
2 Tbsp.	mayonnaise	30 mL
I Tbsp.	fresh basil, chopped	15 mL
I	scallion, sliced	I
I Tbsp.	Dijon mustard	15 mL
I	egg, beaten	I
I pkg.	spring roll wrappers	I pkg.
	corn OR peanut oil for deep-frying	

Preheat the oven to 400°F (200°C).

To make the sauce, rub the tomatoes with a little of the oil. Place in a pan and roast in the oven for ½ hour. Set aside.

In a medium-sized saucepan, heat the rest of the oil, then sauté the onion, garlic and chipotles until tender.

Deglaze the saucepan with the red wine. Add the roasted tomatoes and tomato sauce. Simmer for 45 minutes and pass through a food mill.

To prepare the filling for the spring rolls, mix together the first six ingredients in a large bowl.

Brush the beaten egg over the spring roll wrappers. Place 6 Tbsp. (90 mL) of the filling on each wrapper, fold the sides over, then roll up.

In a deep, heavy-bottomed pot, pour in the oil to a depth of 4 inches (10 cm) and heat to 350°F (180°C).

Deep-fry the spring rolls for 5 to 7 minutes until golden, and serve immediately with the sauce.

Fresh foie gras
with pea tops and rhubarb compote

::

What can you say about foie gras? It's the king of foods, although your doctor might not agree. There is Canadian foie gras available now, so get it fresh if at all possible. Make this in the spring when you can get fresh rhubarb and pea tops. Pea tops are the young shoots growing off the main plant—they are sold in most Asian produce stores. Prepare the compote a day ahead to let the flavours develop. Any leftover rhubarb compote will keep 2 to 4 weeks in the refrigerator. We also serve it with Duck Liver Terrine (page 49).

SERVES 4

RHUBARB COMPOTE

I	lemon, zest and juice	I
¾ cup	rice wine vinegar	200 mL
½ cup	sugar	125 mL
I	garlic clove, minced	I
½ cup	red onion, finely diced	125 mL
I Tbsp.	ginger, peeled and grated	15 mL
3 cups	rhubarb (14 oz./400 g), diced	750 mL

To prepare the compote, combine all the ingredients, except the rhubarb, in a stainless steel pot and bring to a simmer.

Add the rhubarb and simmer for about 20 minutes, until cooked and the mixture thickens. Be careful not to burn the compote. Let cool and refrigerate. Makes 2 cups (500 mL).

FOIE GRAS WITH PEA TOPS

4 3-oz.	slices of fresh foie gras	4 80-g
2 cups	pea tops	500 mL
½ cup	white wine	125 mL
	salt and pepper	
	melba toast	

To prepare the foie gras, heat a heavy-bottomed frying pan or a nonstick pan until it is very, very hot.

While the frying pan is getting hot, add the pea tops and white wine to a saucepan. Cover the pan and place on high heat to steam the pea tops; they take only a few minutes to cook.

Place the slices of foie gras in the very hot frying pan and sear each side for 2 to 3 minutes, until golden and warm. Do not cook for too long, or the liver will just render away. Season.

Arrange the pea tops on plates and place a slice of the foie gras on top. Serve with the rhubarb compote and melba toast.

Chanterelle, goat cheese and pepper strudel

::

Our chanterelle supplier is a Swiss nurse who has a secret patch whose location she won't reveal. She came in for dinner one night and enjoyed the food so much that she offered to bring us chanterelles from her walks in the woods. And we don't need to know where she finds them, as long as she keeps showing up with ten-pound bags. If you don't have your own secret chanterelle supply, morel, shiitake or oyster mushrooms also make an excellent strudel.

SERVES 4

3	red peppers	3
3 Tbsp.	olive oil	45 mL
2	shallots, peeled and thinly sliced	2
I cup	chanterelles	250 mL
	salt and pepper	
I Tbsp.	fresh rosemary leaves, chopped	30 mL
I Tbsp.	fresh parsley, chopped	30 mL
	flour	
10 oz.	puff pastry, fresh OR frozen	300 g
4 Tbsp.	basil pesto (page 151)	60 mL
¾ cup	any kind of soft fresh goat cheese (4 oz./125 g)	180 mL
I	egg, beaten	I
	rock salt for garnish	
	mixed salad greens	

Preheat the oven to 450°F (230°C).

Rub the red peppers with 1 Tbsp. (15 mL) of the olive oil and place in a pan. Roast in the oven for 8 to 10 minutes, turning occasionally, until the skin lifts.

Place the peppers in a bowl and cover tightly with plastic wrap. Let cool for 30 minutes, as this will make it easier to remove the skin. Cut each pepper in quarters, peel off the skin, then remove the core and seeds. Set aside.

Preheat the oven to 350°F (180°C).

In a medium-sized frying pan, heat the rest of the olive oil and sauté the shallots until tender and translucent. Add the chanterelles and sauté until tender. Season, then add the rosemary and parsley. Refrigerate until cold.

On a lightly floured surface, roll out the puff pastry into a rectangle 12 inches (30 cm) wide by 6 inches (15 cm) tall. The thickness should be about ¼ inch (6 mm). The pastry should be cool and the other ingredients should be cold.

Spread the pesto down the centre third of the pastry, leaving a third clear on each side. Lay the quarters of roasted

red pepper on the pesto. Spoon the chanterelle mixture on top of the peppers, then crumble the goat cheese over it.

Fold the left flap of the pastry over the filling to cover it.

Using a pastry cutter or a sharp knife, cut into the right flap of the pastry every ½ inch (1.2 cm).

Brush the top of the folded-over pastry with half of the beaten egg. Fold the strips of pastry over the folded part to form a lattice, pressing lightly to make sure they adhere. Neatly secure all the end pieces under the strudel.

Brush the top of the strudel with the remaining beaten egg. Sprinkle a sparing amount of rock salt on top.

Let the strudel rest for 15 minutes, then place on a baking sheet and bake in the oven for 25 to 33 minutes until golden brown.

Serve slices of the strudel with a small tangle of mixed salad greens.

Eggplant and pepper terrine

Duck liver terrine with rhubarb compote

Poached scallops with black beans and shredded carrot salad

Herbed crêpes stuffed with crabmeat and daikon sprouts

Salmon gravlax with crème fraîche and toasted cornbread

Salmon tartare

Eggplant and pepper terrine

::

Make this terrine the day before you plan to serve it to allow it time to set.
You can also make the terrine in individual moulds instead of a loaf, but that requires a bit more work.

MAKES ONE TERRINE

4	large red peppers	4
4	large yellow peppers	4
1/3 cup	olive oil	100 mL
2	large eggplants	2
1/3 cup	vegetable stock (page 148)	100 mL
2 pkg.	gelatin	2 pkg.
1/4 cup	fresh parsley, chopped	60 mL
1/4 cup	fresh basil, chopped	60 mL

Preheat the oven to 450°F (230°C).

Rub the red and yellow peppers with a little of the olive oil. Place in a pan and roast in the oven for 8 to 10 minutes, turning the peppers every few minutes.

Place the peppers in a bowl and cover tightly with plastic wrap. Let cool for 30 minutes, as this will make it easier to remove the skin. Cut each pepper in half, peel off the skin, then remove the core and seeds.

Peel the eggplants. Cut lengthwise into slices ½ inch (1.2 cm) thick. Sprinkle with salt and let drain on paper towels for 15 minutes.

Brush the eggplant slices with the remaining olive oil. Grill or pan fry over medium heat for 5 to 8 minutes, until golden and tender.

Line a 9 × 5 × 3 inch (25.5 × 9 × 7.5 cm) terrine mould with plastic wrap, using enough to drape well over the sides.

To make the aspic, bring the vegetable stock to a simmer, then stir in the gelatin until dissolved.

The terrine consists of six layers. First layer: arrange half of the red pepper to cover the bottom of the pan, then brush with the aspic. Second layer: use half of the yellow pepper, then brush with the aspic. Third layer: use half of the eggplant and brush with the aspic, then sprinkle with half the parsley and basil. Repeat the three layers of red pepper, yellow pepper and eggplant, brushing aspic on each layer. Sprinkle the rest of the parsley and basil on top.

Once the terrine is assembled, fold the hanging plastic wrap over top of the terrine to seal it. Use a large piece of aluminum foil to cover the top of the terrine.

Balance a 3-pound (1.5-kg) weight on top of the foil on top of the terrine. Place in the refrigerator and let sit overnight.

To serve, turn the mould upside-down so the terrine comes out. Cut into slices with a thin sharp knife while it's still wrapped to help keep it together. Remove the wrapping from the slices before serving.

>
Grilled calamari with sesame soy tomato coulis, page 38

Duck liver terrine with rhubarb compote

::

This is a classic, smooth, puréed terrine. The cognac gives it that perfumed flavour.
You can use fresh chicken or turkey livers in place of duck. As with the foie gras featured in the
Warm Starters section, we pair this terrine with rhubarb compote to cut the richness.

MAKES ONE TERRINE

2-3 Tbsp.	melted butter	30-45 mL
I lb.	duck livers	500 g
²/₃ cup	port	150 mL
9	egg yolks	9
I¹/₂ cups	melted butter	325 mL
I³/₄ cups	double cream	450 mL
¹/₂ cup	cognac	120 mL
¹/₄ tsp.	ground nutmeg	I mL
¹/₂ tsp.	ground white pepper	2 mL
I tsp.	salt	5 mL
	rhubarb compote (page 44)	
	melba toast	

Brush a 10 × 3.5 × 3 inch or 9 × 5 × 3 inch (25.5 × 9 × 7.5 cm) terrine mould with the 2 to 3 Tbsp. (30 to 45 mL) melted butter and chill in the refrigerator.

Clean the livers, then place them in a bowl with the port. Cover and marinate for 6 hours in the refrigerator. Drain the livers and discard the port.

Preheat the oven to 375°F (190°C).

Purée the livers and yolks together in a food processor. Push the mixture through a fine sieve.

Put the liver purée in a bowl. Add the 1½ cups (325 mL) melted butter and cream, whisking well. Add the cognac, nutmeg, white pepper and salt.

Pour the mixture into the terrine mould. Place the mould in a roasting pan, then fill the pan almost up to the top with boiling water. Place this bain-marie in the oven and bake for 40 minutes. When done, remove from the oven and let cool in the bain-marie. Refrigerate overnight.

Use a thin, sharp knife to slice the terrine. Serve with rhubarb compote and melba toast.

<
Asparagus and
minted new potato
salad with sun-dried
tomato mayonnaise,
page 26

Poached scallops
with black beans and shredded carrot salad

::

We use big fat sea scallops with their bright orange roe still attached.
They look stunning served on a bed of black turtle beans.

SERVES 4

BLACK BEANS

½ cup	black turtle beans	125 mL
1 cup	water	250 mL
	vegetable oil	
¼ cup	onion, minced	60 mL
½ tsp.	garlic, minced	2 mL
2 Tbsp.	white wine	30 mL
3 cups	vegetable stock (page 148)	750 mL
	salt and pepper	
¼ cup	sour cream	60 mL
¼ cup	green onions, chopped	60 mL
2 Tbsp.	fresh cilantro, chopped	30 mL

To prepare the black turtle beans, place in a bowl with the water and soak overnight. Drain.

In a saucepan, heat a small amount of vegetable oil and sauté the onion and garlic until tender.

Add the drained beans, white wine and 1 cup (250 mL) of the vegetable stock. Season at this point to ensure that the salt gets right into the beans as they cook. This will reduce the amount of salt necessary to season at the end. Simmer for 40 minutes or until the beans are tender.

Transfer the beans to a shallow dish to let cool. When the beans are cold, mix in the sour cream, green onions and cilantro. Refrigerate until needed.

SHREDDED CARROT SALAD

½ cup	carrot, shredded	125 mL
1 Tbsp.	rice vinegar	15 mL
1 Tbsp.	sesame oil	15 mL

In a bowl, toss the shredded carrot with the rice vinegar and sesame oil.

1	lemon, halved	1
	salt	
1 lb.	sea scallops	500 g
1 tsp.	sesame seeds	5 mL

To prepare the scallops, place the lemon halves in a saucepan with the remaining 2 cups (500 mL) of the vegetable stock, and bring to a simmer over medium heat. Add salt to taste.

Add the scallops to the simmering stock. Once the mixture begins to boil again, remove from the heat. Allow the scallops to cool in the liquid, then place the scallops (still in the liquid) in the refrigerator.

To serve, spread a pool of the bean mixture on a plate and place a small mound of shredded carrot salad in the centre. Arrange the scallops on the beans in a circle around the carrot mixture. Garnish with a sprinkle of sesame seeds.

Herbed crêpes
stuffed with crabmeat and daikon sprouts

::

*Daikon sprouts are also called radish sprouts. The sharp taste of the sprouts works well
with the sweetness of the crab. When you make the crêpes, don't refrigerate them, or they will dry out.*

SERVES 4

CRABMEAT AND DAIKON FILLING

I	red pepper	I
	vegetable oil	
I lb.	fresh crabmeat	500 g
2	avocados, peeled and sliced	2
½ cup	daikon sprouts	125 mL
16	chives	16

Preheat the oven to 450°F (230°C).

Rub the red pepper with a little vegetable oil and place in
a pan. Roast in the oven for 8 to 10 minutes, turning
occasionally, until the skin lifts.

Place the pepper in a bowl and cover tightly with plastic
wrap. Let cool for 30 minutes, as this will make it easier
to remove the skin. Cut the pepper in half, peel off the
skin, then remove the core and seeds. Slice thinly.

HERBED CRÊPES

I cup	flour	250 mL
I Tbsp.	fresh dill, chopped	15 mL
I Tbsp.	fresh chives, chopped	15 mL
I Tbsp.	fresh parsley, chopped	15 mL
	salt and pepper	
2	eggs	2
1¾ cups	milk	425 mL
2 Tbsp.	butter, melted	30 mL

To make the crepes, mix together the flour, dill, chives,
parsley, salt and pepper in a bowl.

In another bowl, beat together the eggs and milk. Add to
the dry ingredients and whisk until well combined. Whisk
in the melted butter. Allow the batter to rest 30 minutes
before using.

In a seasoned crêpe pan or nonstick frying pan, make 8
crêpes using ¼ cup (60 mL) of batter for each. Spread the
batter thinly by rolling it around the pan to coat it. Cook
each crêpe until it is dry around the edges and lightly
coloured on the bottom, then turn it over and cook until
the same on the other side. Place the crêpes on parchment
paper to prevent sticking.

To assemble the crêpes, lay out each one with the good
side down, and arrange the fillings in rows lengthwise as
follows: ⅛ of the crab, ⅛ of the roasted red pepper, ⅛ of
the avocado, ⅛ of the sprouts and 2 chives. Roll up each
crepe as tightly as possible without tearing.

Slice each crêpe into 4 to 5 rounds and arrange flat on
plates.

Salmon gravlax
with crème fraîche and toasted cornbread

::

*This recipe is a southern hemisphere interpretation of the traditional gravlax recipe.
Michael Allemeier loves using spices. His background is German and he spent a lot of time in South Africa,
where coriander seed is a predominant flavour in the cooking. You can use fresh salmon for this dish,
even though it's uncooked. The salt cure will kill any bacteria or parasites.*

SERVES 4

GRAVLAX

2 lbs.	side of salmon, skin left on	1 kg
¾ cup	salt	250 g
1¾ cup	sugar	375 g
3 Tbsp.	coriander seeds	45 mL
4 Tbsp.	juniper berries	60 mL
3 Tbsp.	fennel seeds	45 mL
2 Tbsp.	black peppercorns	30 mL

The side of salmon must still have the skin left on. Remove the pin bones and any belly bones. Clean off the fat.

Mix the salt and sugar together in a bowl.

To prepare the curing mixture, grind the coriander, juniper berries, fennel and peppercorns in a coffee grinder until quite fine. Add to the salt and sugar and mix well.

Place the salmon, skin side down, in a baking dish. Pour the curing mixture over the salmon to completely cover it.

Cover the dish with plastic wrap and place in the refrigerator for 24 hours.

Remove the salmon from the curing mixture, turn it over, then cover the salmon with the curing mixture. Refrigerate for a second 24 hours.

Remove the salmon from the curing mixture, turn it over, then cover the salmon with the curing mixture. Refrigerate for a third 24 hours.

Remove the salmon from the cure. Under cold running water, quickly rinse off the curing mixture. Pat dry with paper towels. Place in a dish and leave uncovered in the refrigerator for 24 hours to dry out the surface.

CRÈME FRAÎCHE

1 cup	whipping cream	250 mL
1 Tbsp.	buttermilk	15 mL

To make the crème fraîche, mix together the whipping cream and buttermilk in a bowl. Cover the bowl with plastic wrap and leave out in a warm place for 2 to 3 days, until thickened to the consistency of yogurt. Refrigerate until needed. Makes 1 cup (250 mL).

	cornbread, toasted (page 142)
	watercress
	lemon wedges

To serve the gravlax, slice it thinly and arrange on plates. Serve with the crème fraîche and toasted cornbread. Garnish with watercress and lemon wedges.

Salmon tartare

::

*For this uncured raw salmon dish, the salmon must be as fresh as possible and frozen overnight,
then allowed to thaw in the fridge. Salmon that has been flash-frozen on the boat
is even better, because it is frozen at a much lower temperature than a home freezer can reach.
Freezing kills any bacteria or parasites that might be present.*

SERVES 4

	crushed ice	
9 oz.	salmon, skin and bones removed	250 g
½ cup	red onion, finely diced	125 mL
20	capers, finely chopped	20
I	garlic clove, finely chopped	I
½ cup	fresh parsley, chopped	125 mL
2 Tbsp.	fresh dill, finely chopped	30 mL
2 tsp.	Dijon mustard	10 mL
3 Tbsp.	mayonnaise	45 mL
10 drops	Tabasco sauce	10 drops
½ tsp.	Worcestershire sauce	2 mL
I Tbsp.	fresh lemon juice	15 mL
	salt and black pepper	
	melba toast OR fresh bread	

Place the crushed ice in a large bowl. Place a smaller bowl in the ice so that the contents of the inner bowl will remain cool. Refrigerate until needed.

With a very sharp knife, cube the salmon. Chop up the cubes until the fish is quite minced.

Put the minced salmon in the smaller bowl placed in the crushed ice.

In another bowl, combine the red onion, capers, garlic, parsley, dill and mustard. Fold into the minced salmon in the bowl placed in the crushed ice. Add the mayonnaise, Tabasco, Worcestershire and fresh lemon juice. Fold all the ingredients together and season.

Serve within an hour with melba toast or fresh bread.

Barbecued oyster brochettes with tamarind sauce

Breaded razor clams with black olive aïoli

Crabcakes with sun-dried tomato chutney

Pan-seared scallops with lemongrass and chervil sauce

Whole crab hot pot with green onions and ginger

Oyster, artichoke, lemon zest and chive stew

Split prawns roasted with thyme and garlic butter

Cornmeal-crusted prawns seared in peanut oil with mustard seed sauce

Clams on the beach

Barbecued oyster brochettes
with tamarind sauce

::

The flavour of tamarind goes perfectly with oysters—one of those uncanny flavour combinations.
Tamarind is readily available in Asian food stores.
Oysters cooked on the barbecue are a treat, especially if you're grilling them over wood.
Find the biggest, fattest beach oysters you can.
We poach them first to facilitate skewering and to give them a good texture.

SERVES 4

TAMARIND SAUCE

4 cups	cold water	I L
8 oz.	dried tamarind	225 g
1¼ cups	white wine	300 mL
3	shallots, finely diced	3
I cup	whipping cream	250 mL
	salt and pepper	

To prepare the sauce, add the water and dried tamarind to a saucepan. Bring to a boil and stir to break up the tamarind. Simmer for 30 minutes, stirring every 10 minutes.

Strain the tamarind stock through a sieve, pushing the contents through with the back of a spoon. Discard any seeds.

To a large frying pan, add the white wine and the shallots. Reduce the wine by half. Then add 2 cups (500 mL) of the tamarind stock and reduce by half.

Add the whipping cream and bring to a simmer. Strain the sauce and adjust the seasoning. Keep warm or refrigerate until needed.

BARBECUED OYSTER BROCHETTES

8 cups	water	2 L
24	large beach oysters, shucked	24
2 Tbsp.	canola oil	30 mL

Preheat the barbecue.

To prepare the oysters, bring the water to a boil in a large pot. Add the oysters and bring back to a simmer. Remove the oysters from the water and let cool.

Thread the oysters on eight bamboo skewers that are 6 inches (15 cm) long.

Brush the oyster brochettes with the canola oil and grill over medium heat for 3 minutes per side. Serve with the tamarind sauce.

Wine suggestion
Champagne or a sparkling wine

Breaded razor clams
with black olive aïoli

::

To test the freshness of razor clams, touch the neck that sticks out of the shell—if it moves, the clam is alive. Discard all dead clams. The same test works for geoducks, which can be used instead of the razor clams in this recipe.

If you cannot obtain sun-dried black olives, substitute oil-cured black olives.

SERVES 4

BLACK OLIVE AÏOLI

2	egg yolks	2
12	sun-dried black olives	12
I	garlic clove	I
I tsp.	Dijon mustard	5 mL
I	lemon	I
I cup	canola oil	250 mL
½ cup	olive oil	125 mL

To prepare the aïoli, place the egg yolks, olives, garlic and mustard in a food processor, then purée.

Zest and juice the lemon, then finely chop the zest. Add the juice and the zest to the egg yolk mixture, then purée.

In a separate bowl, mix together the canola and olive oils.

With the food processor's motor running, slowly add the oil to the egg yolk mixture, drop by drop (adding the oil too quickly can cause the aïoli to separate). After adding 25 per cent of the oil, add the rest of the oil a little more quickly. Refrigerate until needed.

	corn oil for deep-frying	
12	razor clams	12
½ cup	white wine	125 mL
3	eggs	3
I cup	flour	250 mL
2 cups	fine breadcrumbs	500 mL

Preheat the oil in the deep fryer to 350°F (180°C).

To prepare the clams, place them with the white wine in a covered pot. Over medium heat, steam the clams for 5 to 10 minutes, until they open.

As soon as the clams open, remove them from the pot. Let them cool, then shuck. Use a pair of kitchen scissors to cut out the stomach, which is a black sack about halfway up the body. It must be removed because it has a nasty taste.

Place the eggs, flour and breadcrumbs in three separate bowls. Beat the eggs.

Roll each clam in the flour, then dip it in the beaten eggs, making sure to coat it well. Drain the clam and roll it in the breadcrumbs to ensure an even coating.

Deep-fry the clams for 4 to 5 minutes until golden brown. Serve with the black olive aïoli.

Wine suggestion
A rosé from Provence

Crabcakes with sun-dried tomato chutney

::

This crabcake recipe is one of our signature dishes. We've served crabcakes with a number of different condiments, but the sun-dried tomato chutney is a favourite. Its piquancy balances the sweetness of the crabcakes. Although there doesn't appear to be a lot of sun-dried tomato in the recipe, it's enough. Make the chutney the day before for better flavour. Instead of the chutney, you can serve the crabcakes with Red Pepper Mayonnaise (page 77).

SERVES 4

SUN-DRIED TOMATO CHUTNEY

1-inch	piece of ginger, peeled	2.5-cm
2	garlic cloves	2
1	large shallot	1
1 cup	fennel bulb, finely diced	250 mL
3 Tbsp.	lemon juice	50 mL
½ cup	white wine vinegar	120 mL
¾ cup	sugar	180 mL
1 cup	roma tomatoes, cored and diced	250 mL
2 Tbsp.	sun-dried tomatoes, quartered	30 mL
1 stick	cinnamon	1 stick
1 piece	allspice	1 piece
1	clove	1

To prepare the chutney, combine the ginger, garlic, shallot, fennel and lemon juice in a food processor and grind to a paste. Set aside.

In a heavy stainless steel pot, combine the vinegar and sugar. Bring to a simmer. Add the roma tomatoes, sun-dried tomatoes, cinnamon, allspice and clove, then bring to a simmer while stirring. Add the ginger paste and mix well. Simmer for 30 to 40 minutes until thick, watching to make sure the chutney doesn't burn.

Pour the chutney into a clean covered container and refrigerate—it is best if left to sit for one day before serving. Makes 2 cups (500 mL).

Do not freeze leftover chutney—it will keep for 3 to 4 weeks in the refrigerator. It's also good served with steamed greens, especially pea tops.

CRABCAKES

I lb.	Dungeness crabmeat, cooked	500 g
I cup	fresh breadcrumbs	250 mL
⅓ cup	green onions, thinly sliced	75 mL
I	red pepper, seeded, cored and diced	I
4 Tbsp.	mayonnaise	60 mL
	salt and pepper	
I Tbsp.	vegetable oil	15 mL

Preheat the oven to 350°F (180°C).

To prepare the crabcakes, mix together the crabmeat, breadcrumbs, green onions, red pepper and mayonnaise in a bowl. As crabmeat can vary in saltiness, adjust the salt and pepper to taste. Form the mixture into 8 crabcakes.

In a nonstick frying pan, heat the vegetable oil. Brown the crabcakes over medium heat, until golden on both sides.

Transfer the crabcakes to a baking sheet and place in the oven for 5 minutes, until heated through.

Place two crabcakes on each plate and serve with the chutney.

Wine suggestion
A tropical-flavoured Chardonnay from Australia

Pan-seared scallops with
lemongrass and chervil sauce

::

This signature dish by Michael Allemeier was on the first menu he created for Bishop's and has been on it ever since. We serve it with Crisp Potato Pancakes (page 121). If you can't get fresh chervil for the sauce, substitute fennel tops or tarragon. We have one customer who, every time she orders this dish, comes roaring into the kitchen, saying, "I must have a jar of this sauce in my fridge at all times!"

SERVES 4

LEMONGRASS AND CHERVIL SAUCE

½ cup	shallots, chopped	125 mL
½ cup	lemon juice	125 mL
¾ cup	lemongrass, chopped	200 mL
1 cup	white wine	250 mL
2 cups	heavy cream	500 mL
pinch	salt	pinch
pinch	pepper	pinch
2 Tbsp.	fresh chervil, chopped fine	30 mL
2 Tbsp.	tomato, seeded and finely diced	30 mL

To prepare the sauce, combine the shallots, lemon juice and lemongrass in a stainless steel saucepan. Bring to a boil and reduce until the liquid just covers the bottom of the pan. Add the white wine and reduce by half. Add the heavy cream and bring to a boil. Strain immediately and season. Set aside until the scallops are cooked. (The recipe can be prepared up to this point in advance.)

To complete the sauce, bring it back to a simmer, add the chervil and tomato, then remove from heat.

1 Tbsp.	vegetable oil	15 mL
24	large scallops (24 oz./700 g)	24
pinch	salt	pinch
pinch	freshly ground pepper	pinch

To prepare the scallops, add the oil to a frying pan over medium-high heat. Blot the scallops on a paper towel to help prevent splattering, then place gently in the pan and sear for 1 to 2 minutes, until golden brown. Turn over and season, then cook for 1 minute longer, or until slightly firm to the touch.

Remove the scallops from the pan and blot them on a paper towel to avoid discolouring the sauce.

To serve, spread the bottom of each plate with enough sauce to cover it. Arrange 6 scallops on each plate in a circle about one inch (2.5 cm) from the rim of the plate. Place a crisp potato pancake on top of the scallops.

Wine suggestion
A Pinot Gris or Pinot Blanc from the Pacific Northwest

Whole crab hot pot
with green onions and ginger

::

A casual dish to enjoy with some very close friends.
Tuck the tablecloth around yourselves and just spend a couple of hours cracking and eating the crabs.

You will need four Chinese hot pots, which are ceramic with tight-fitting lids and can be
used for both cooking and serving. They are readily available from any Chinese cooking shop.

SERVES 4

4	**Dungeness crabs**	4
2 Tbsp.	sesame oil	30 mL
½ cup	red onion, diced	125 mL
I Tbsp.	garlic, minced	15 mL
I Tbsp.	ginger, peeled and grated	15 mL
I	jalapeño pepper, minced (optional)	I
I ½ cups	tomatoes, diced	375 mL
2 cups	fish OR crab stock (page 147)	500 mL
I cup	green onions, sliced	250 mL

Bring a large pot of water to a boil. Throw in the crabs one at a time and bring to a simmer. DO NOT BOIL. Each crab should cook for 8 minutes per pound. Remove and let cool.

To clean a crab, clasp it from the back and pry off the top shell, then set that aside. Under cold running water, remove all the organs and innards attached to the crab's body, including the triangular plate located on its underside. Rinse the top shell under cold running water, until clean and free of all innards.

Add the sesame oil to a frying pan over medium heat. Add the onion and sauté until tender. Add the garlic and ginger, cooking until fragrant, being careful not to burn them. Add the jalapeño pepper (optional), tomatoes and fish (or crab) stock. Simmer for 30 minutes.

Place each cleaned crab in a Chinese ceramic hot pot. Cover with the stock mixture and add the green onions.

Place each hot pot on its own stove burner or element over medium-high heat. Bring to a simmer, then cover and cook for 5 minutes. Place each hot pot on a plate and serve at once.

Wine suggestion
A young white Burgundy

Oyster, artichoke, lemon zest and chive stew

::

Rich and hearty, this dish is perfect for West Coast winters—cheering on a rainy day.
A good white wine and a baguette are all it needs.
The sauce can be varied according to preference by allowing the cream to reduce to the desired thickness.
A thinner variation makes an excellent rich soup, while a slightly thicker version is a delicious
starter or lunch dish: try serving it over a piece of toast with some fresh Parmesan cheese grated on top.

SERVES 4

2 cups	fresh shucked oysters	500 mL
2 Tbsp.	butter	30 mL
1 14-oz. can	artichoke hearts, drained and halved	1 398-mL can
2 Tbsp.	lemon zest, grated	30 mL
¼ cup	white wine	60 mL
1½ cups	heavy cream	375 mL
¼ cup	fresh chives, chopped	60 mL
	salt and pepper	

Remove the oysters from their juice and reserve the liquid. In a saucepan, melt the butter and sauté the oysters for 1 minute or so, until they just begin to plump up.

Add the artichokes, lemon zest, white wine, heavy cream and any reserved juice from the oysters. Bring to a boil, then simmer for about 5 minutes, until the oysters are slightly firm to the touch. Add the chives, season and serve.

Note: We use fresh artichokes in the restaurant, but it takes two people a couple of hours to prepare them. The canned product is very good and a lot less work. If you're ambitious and want to use fresh artichokes, buy about 20 small ones. Trim off all the outside leaves until you get to the yellow-green heart. In a large pot, make acidulated water by combining 7 Tbsp. (100 mL) lemon juice (or white vinegar) with 4 cups (1 L) water and bring to a boil. Add the artichokes and simmer for 6 to 7 minutes until cooked.

Wine suggestion
A rich buttery Chardonnay

Split prawns
roasted with thyme and garlic butter

::

Roasting crustaceans in the shell brings out much more flavour than cooking them peeled. We split the prawns to make it easy to remove the meat from the shells after cooking. Remember to save the shells (and heads, if any) for Shellfish Stock (page 147) or Prawn Bisque (page 18).

Try to get spot prawns, a West Coast species with sweet-tasting flesh, easily identified by the two white spots at the top of the tail. If you buy prawns with the heads on, watch out for any that are black at the base of the head, as this means the flesh will be mushy. If you can't find spot prawns, look for a flavourful variety, such as Louisiana bay shrimp, since the delicate flavour of the prawn is the focus of this dish.

SERVES 4

¼ cup	fresh thyme sprigs	60 mL
½ cup	butter	125 mL
2	garlic cloves, sliced	2
1½ lbs.	fresh prawn tails in shell	750 g

Preheat the oven to 400°F (200°C).

Pick the leaves off the thyme and set aside. Roughly chop the stems and set aside separately.

In a saucepan over medium-low heat, melt the butter, then add the chopped thyme stems and garlic. Simmer until all milk products evaporate and only the clarified butterfat remains. Strain.

Split the prawns down the back and open them, but leave them in their shells. Remove and discard any veins.

Lay out the prawns on a baking sheet and brush with the thyme- and garlic-scented clarified butter. Sprinkle the thyme leaves over the prawns. Roast in the oven for 2 to 5 minutes (depending on size), until the prawns turn pink. Serve at once.

Wine suggestion
A crisp Fumé Blanc from New Zealand

Cornmeal-crusted prawns
seared in peanut oil with mustard seed sauce

::

In the restaurant, we serve these prawns on a bed of steamed greens (such as kale, mustard greens, etc.) drizzled with the sauce, like a warm salad. We top it with crispy shoestring potatoes. The prawns and sauce are also delicious served as an hors d'oeuvre.

SERVES 4

1 ½ lbs.	prawn tails	750 g
½ cup	buttermilk	125 mL

Peel and devein the prawn tails. Place them in a bowl with the buttermilk and marinate in the refrigerator for 1 to 2 hours.

MUSTARD SEED SAUCE

½ cup	shallots, diced	125 mL
½ cup	white wine vinegar	125 mL
1 cup	white wine	250 mL
1 cup	fish stock (page 147)	250 mL
2 Tbsp.	mustard seeds	30 mL
2 Tbsp.	Dijon mustard	30 mL
2 Tbsp.	grainy mustard	30 mL
¼ cup	olive oil	60 mL

To prepare the sauce, combine the shallots and vinegar in a saucepan. Over medium heat, reduce until the liquid just covers the bottom of the pan. Add the white wine and reduce by half. Add the fish stock and reduce by half.

Lightly toast the mustard seeds in a dry frying pan over medium heat for 1 minute. Put the mustard seeds and both types of mustard into a food processor. With the motor running, slowly add the reduced stock. When all the stock has been incorporated, slowly pour in the olive oil and process until well combined. Return the sauce to the saucepan and keep warm.

½ cup	rice flour	125 mL
1 cup	cornmeal	250 mL
pinch	salt and freshly ground pepper	pinch
1 cup	peanut oil for frying	250 mL

Preheat the oven to 300°F (150°C).

To prepare the coating, combine the rice flour and cornmeal in a bowl. Season with a pinch each of salt and pepper.

Remove the prawns from the buttermilk, shaking off any excess. Dredge them in the cornmeal mixture, coating evenly.

To a large frying pan, add peanut oil to a depth of ¼ inch (6 mm) and heat. Over medium-high heat, fry the prawns in batches for 1 to 2 minutes per side, until the flesh turns pink and slightly firm.

Keep the cooked prawns warm in the oven until all of them are ready. Serve with the sauce on the side.

Wine suggestion
A spicy Gewürztraminer

Clams on the beach

::

We made this dish once for a special function on a yacht. Cherrystone clams are about the size of a tennis ball. The clam meat mixed with the ratatouille-style filling looks colourful and inviting stuffed back in the shells and served on a "beach" of sand or rock salt. You can sterilize the sand in the oven by baking it for 20 minutes at 450°F (230°C).

SERVES 4

4	cherrystone clams	4
2 Tbsp.	olive oil	30 mL
2	shallots, finely diced	2
I	garlic clove, finely diced	I
½ cup	zucchini, diced	125 mL
½ cup	tomatoes, diced	125 mL
¼ cup	fresh breadcrumbs	60 mL
½ cup	Parmesan cheese, grated	125 mL
¼ cup	fresh parsley, chopped	60 mL
	salt and pepper	

Preheat the oven to 400°F (200°C).

Arrange the clams on a baking sheet and place in the oven for 5 to 20 minutes until they open. Remove from the oven and let cool.

Pry open the clams and use a spoon to scrape out all the meat. Save any liquid. Clean the shells and save them. Chop up the meat coarsely.

In a frying pan, heat the olive oil, then sauté the shallots and garlic until tender. Add the zucchini and sauté for 3 minutes. Add the tomatoes and any juice saved from the clams, then simmer for 15 minutes.

Add the clam meat, breadcrumbs and half the Parmesan cheese. Simmer for 5 minutes, then let cool. Add the chopped parsley and season.

Spoon the clam mixture back into the shells and cover with the remaining Parmesan cheese. Place the stuffed clams on a baking sheet in the oven for 15 minutes until hot.

Serve on a bed of clean sea sand or coarse rock salt.

Wine suggestion
A Pinot Blanc or a rich Sylvaner from Alsace

Roast halibut fillet with red onion and strawberry salsa

Poached salmon with leek and chive sauce

Pan-roasted red snapper with goat cheese fritters and braised endive

Ale-battered sole with lime crème fraîche

Steamed salmon fillet with blood orange and ginger sauce

Whole fried rock cod in spicy ginger, scallion and red currant broth

Grilled white spring salmon with red currant and green peppercorn salsa

Grilled tuna with gazpacho salsa

Tandoori halibut cheeks

Smoked Alaska black cod with sun-dried pepper sabayon

Roast ling cod with garlic mashed potatoes

Steamed sablefish with lobster and vanilla bean sauce

Roast halibut fillet
with red onion and strawberry salsa

::

The combination of halibut and strawberries is a natural one,
since they arrive in the market at the same time. Instead of roasting the halibut in the oven,
you can barbecue it, but be careful not to overcook the fish.

SERVES 4

RED ONION AND STRAWBERRY SALSA		
2 cups	strawberries, diced	500 mL
⅓ cup	sweet red onion, finely diced	75 mL
4 Tbsp.	fresh lime juice	60 mL
3 Tbsp.	fresh orange juice	50 mL
2 Tbsp.	fresh mint, chopped	25 mL

1 Tbsp.	canola oil	15 mL
4 7-oz.	pieces of halibut	4 200-g
	salt and pepper	

To prepare the salsa, combine the strawberries, onion, lime juice, orange juice and mint in a stainless steel or ceramic bowl. Cover with plastic wrap and let sit at room temperature for 1 hour. Serve or refrigerate until needed (always serve the salsa at room temperature).

Preheat the oven to 350°F (180°C).

Add the canola oil to a nonstick frying pan over medium heat and brown the halibut on each side.

Place the halibut on a baking sheet and roast in the oven for 8 to 12 minutes, until it feels firm to the touch. Season with salt and pepper. Serve at once with the salsa.

Wine suggestion
A grassy Sauvignon Blanc from California or Chile

Poached salmon
with leek and chive sauce

::

This dish can be served either cold or warm.
Do not allow the poaching liquid to boil, as the salmon tastes better when simmered.
And use only the white part of the leek for the sauce.

SERVES 4

LEEK AND CHIVE SAUCE

2 tsp.	butter	10 mL
1 cup	leeks, diced	250 mL
¼ cup	celery, diced	60 mL
¾ cup	dry white wine	180 mL
1	bay leaf	1
2 cups	fish stock (page 147)	500 mL
3 Tbsp.	whipping cream	45 mL

4 7-oz.	salmon fillets	4 200-g
8 cups	vegetable stock (page 148)	2 L
1	lemon	1
2 Tbsp.	fresh chives, finely chopped	30 mL

To prepare the sauce, melt the butter in a frying pan over medium heat, then sauté the leeks and celery for 7 to 9 minutes, until tender. Add the white wine and bay leaf, then reduce to ⅓. Add the fish stock and reduce to ⅓. Add the cream and bring to a simmer.

Remove the bay leaf. Purée the sauce in a blender or food processor. Pass through a sieve. Keep the sauce warm while you prepare the salmon.

Place the salmon fillets and vegetable stock in a large flat saucepan. Cut the lemon in half and squeeze the juice into the stock, then add the lemon halves.

Over medium heat, bring the salmon to a simmer (do not let it boil) and poach for 3 to 4 minutes. Remove the pan from the heat and let the salmon sit in the stock for 2 minutes.

Remove and discard the lemon halves. Carefully remove the salmon fillets, arrange on plates and serve with the sauce. Garnish with a sprinkling of the chives.

Wine suggestion
A young, light Pinot Noir

Pan-roasted red snapper
with goat cheese fritters and braised endive

::

Snapper is a delicate fish that can fall apart easily.
If you scale the skin and leave it attached, the fish will not only hold together better but also retain more flavour.
To scale the fish, scrape the back of a knife against the grain of the scales.

SERVES 4

VINAIGRETTE

⅓ cup	tarragon vinegar	80 mL
½ cup	hazelnut oil	125 mL
½ cup	vegetable oil	125 mL
	salt and pepper	

To prepare the vinaigrette, place the tarragon vinegar, hazelnut and vegetable oils in a small bowl and whisk together. Season to taste.

GOAT CHEESE FRITTERS

	corn OR peanut oil for deep-frying	
½ cup	soft goat cheese	125 mL
3	eggs	3
I cup	flour	250 mL
I tsp.	baking powder	5 mL
I Tbsp.	fresh parsley	15 mL
	salt and pepper	

In a deep, heavy-bottomed pot, pour in the oil to a depth of 4 inches (10 cm) and heat to 350°F (180°C).

To prepare the fritter batter, mix together the goat cheese and eggs in a food processor. Add the flour, baking powder and parsley, mixing until just combined. The mixture should be the consistency of muffin batter; if it is too thick, thin it with a little milk. Season.

To cook the fritters, drop the batter 1 Tbsp. (15 mL) at a time into the oil and fry for 2 to 3 minutes, until golden brown. Drain the fritters on paper towels, place on a baking sheet and keep warm in a low oven.

	salt and pepper	
I ½ lbs.	red snapper fillets	750 g
	vegetable oil	
I head	curly endive	I head

Season the red snapper fillets. In a nonstick frying pan, heat a little bit of vegetable oil and sauté the snapper for 2½ to 3½ minutes per side until done. Cover the pan to create a miniature oven on top of the stove, searing the outside of the fish to a golden crust while steaming it in its own juices. Keep the temperature medium-high to generate enough heat to cook the fish evenly.

Place the endive in a covered saucepan with a little bit of water and steam it for 1 to 2 minutes until it wilts. Drain.

To assemble, place the endive leaves on the plates. Drizzle with some vinaigrette and top with the snapper. Garnish with the goat cheese fritters.

Wine suggestion
A Gewürztraminer from Alsace or the Pacific Northwest

Ale-battered sole
with lime crème fraîche

::

Bishop's version of fish and chips—but without the chips. The batter recipe has been passed down through the English side of Michael Allemeier's family. Use a good dark beer for the batter. Michael makes his own beer and ale at home with a kit that was a wedding gift, and he thanks his former sous-chef, who gave it to them.

The metric measures given for the batter are more precise than those given in imperial. To achieve the best results, try using the metric measures. Note that some of these are by weight, which is more dependable and accurate than volume, so watch out for them and use a kitchen scale calibrated in metric.

SERVES 4

LIME CRÈME FRAÎCHE

1 cup	whipping cream	250 mL
1 Tbsp.	buttermilk	15 mL
3	limes	3

To prepare the crème fraîche, combine the whipping cream and the buttermilk in a bowl. Cover the bowl with plastic wrap and leave in a warm place for 2 to 3 days, until the cream reaches the consistency of thick yogurt.

Zest and juice the limes. Mix the zest and juice with the crème fraîche. Refrigerate until needed. Makes 1 cup (250 mL).

ALE BATTER

3 cups	flour	450 g
1 tsp.	salt	10 g
1 Tbsp.	sugar	15 g
2 cups	dark beer	500 mL
4	egg yolks	4
¼ cup	melted butter	100 g
5	egg whites	5

To make the batter, sift together the flour, salt and sugar in a bowl. Add the beer and egg yolks, mixing until smooth and homogenized. Slowly whisk in the melted butter.

In another bowl, whisk the egg whites to light peaks. Fold the egg whites into the batter mixture and let ferment in a warm place for 30 minutes. Punch down. The batter is now ready to use and will be good for a few hours.

½ cup	vegetable oil	125 mL
	salt and pepper	
8 3½-oz.	sole fillets	8 100-g

Heat the vegetable oil in a large frying pan over medium heat. The oil should be only about ⅓ inch (8 mm) deep, as the fish is not deep-fried.

Season the sole fillets and dip into the batter one at a time. Place the fish in the frying pan and cook for 4 to 5 minutes per side, until golden brown.

Place two sole fillets on each plate and serve with the lime crème fraîche.

Beverage suggestion
A British ale

Steamed salmon fillet
with blood orange and ginger sauce

::

You will need a Chinese bamboo steamer to cook the fish. The sauce is a variation on sauce maltaise, which is hollandaise flavoured with blood oranges. The blood oranges we get in North America aren't as tasty as the ones in the Mediterranean, so if you find the blood orange juice a bit bland, mix in some regular orange juice. If blood oranges aren't available, use regular orange juice.

SERVES 4

BLOOD ORANGE AND GINGER SAUCE

½ cup	blood orange juice	125 mL
2 Tbsp.	rice vinegar	30 mL
1 tsp.	ginger, peeled and grated	5 mL
½ tsp.	garlic, minced	2 mL
¼ cup	white wine	60 mL
2	egg yolks	2
½ cup	butter, softened	125 mL
	salt and pepper	

To make the sauce, mix together the orange juice, vinegar, grated ginger, garlic and white wine in a nonreactive saucepan. Bring to a boil and reduce to ¼ cup (60 mL). Strain.

In a stainless steel bowl over simmering water, whisk together the egg yolks and the reduced orange juice mixture, until pale, hot and slightly thickened. Whisk in the butter 1 Tbsp. (15 mL) at a time, until it is all incorporated. Season to taste and keep the sauce at room temperature while the salmon is cooking.

1 2-inch	piece of ginger, sliced	1 5-cm
4 7-oz.	salmon fillets	4 200-g
	sea salt and freshly ground pepper	

To prepare the salmon, bring water to a simmer in a large pot and add the sliced ginger. Place the salmon fillets in the bamboo steamer, place over the ginger water and cook for 8 minutes or until done. Season with salt and pepper. (When cooking fish in a bamboo steamer, season *after* it is done so that less of the milky white protein is released.)

Place the salmon fillets on plates and spoon the sauce over top.

Wine suggestion
A rich, oaky Chardonnay

>
Salmon gravlax,
page 52, and
Salmon tartare,
page 54, with
toasted cornbread,

Whole fried rock cod
in spicy ginger, scallion and red currant broth

::

Fish cooked whole is much more flavourful than a fillet, and the crispy skin is a beautiful contrast with the tender flesh. Ask your fishmonger to gut and scale the fish but to leave it whole with the head and tail on. The type of rock cod we use at the restaurant is either a quillback or a china stripe.

SERVES 4

SPICY GINGER, SCALLION AND RED CURRANT BROTH

2 Tbsp.	sesame oil	30 mL
4 Tbsp.	ginger, peeled and grated	60 mL
1 cup	red onion, finely diced	250 mL
½ cup	carrot, finely diced	125 mL
½ cup	celery, finely diced	125 mL
¼ cup	fennel bulb, finely diced	60 mL
1	jalapeño pepper, diced	1
1 cup	red wine	250 mL
2 cups	fish stock (page 147)	500 mL
1 cup	green onions, sliced	250 mL
½ cup	red currants	125 mL

4 10-14 oz.	whole rock cod, cleaned and scaled	4 300-400 g
1 cup	cornstarch	250 mL
1 cup	peanut oil	250 mL
	salt and pepper	

To prepare the broth, heat the sesame oil in a large saucepan, then sauté the ginger and red onion until tender. Add the carrot, celery, fennel and jalapeño, then sweat for 3 to 4 minutes.

Add the red wine and reduce by half. Add the fish stock and simmer for 20 minutes. Strain and keep warm.

Reserve the green onions and red currants to add to the broth just before serving.

<
Whole fried rock
cod in spicy ginger,
scallion and red
currant broth

Preheat the oven to 375°F (190°C).

Roll each whole fish in the cornstarch to coat it evenly and shake off the excess.

In a large frying pan, heat the peanut oil until it becomes very hot (a drop of water should spit out in a few seconds).

Carefully place the cod in the hot oil and brown on both sides. Take care when turning over the fish not to tear the skin or splash yourself with hot oil.

When the fish are browned, place on a baking sheet and roast in the oven for 5 to 6 minutes until done. Season well and keep warm in the oven.

To serve, finish the hot broth by adding the green onions and red currants. Place each cod in a bowl with some broth.

Wine suggestion
A medium-dry Riesling

Grilled white spring salmon
with red currant and green peppercorn salsa

::

White spring is a salmon that fishermen used to keep for themselves.
Because of the white flesh, the price is usually lower despite the good flavour.
The high fat content makes it suitable for grilling because it doesn't dry out.
If red currants are not available, substitute raspberries.

SERVES 4

RED CURRANT AND GREEN PEPPERCORN SALSA		
I cup	red currants	250 mL
½ cup	red onion, finely diced	125 mL
2 Tbsp.	green peppercorns	30 mL
2 Tbsp.	fresh lemon juice	30 mL
2 Tbsp.	fresh mint leaves, chopped	30 mL
2 Tbsp.	olive oil	30 mL
¼ cup	white wine	60 mL

To prepare the salsa, combine all the ingredients in a bowl. Set aside until needed.

	salt and pepper	
I½ lbs.	white spring salmon fillets	750 g

Season the salmon fillets, then grill for 3½ to 5 minutes per side until just done. Place on plates.

Warm the salsa by tossing it in a hot frying pan until fragrant, then spoon it over the salmon.

Wine suggestion
A rich, concentrated, dry Riesling

Grilled tuna with gazpacho salsa

::

A refreshing combination for summertime. Buy the tuna as thick as possible—no less than 1 inch (2.5 cm).
The secret to keeping tuna moist is to cook it at very high heat for a short time.
If your barbecue isn't very hot, put some foil over it for 10 to 20 minutes while it's preheating.

SERVES 4

4	tomatoes, peeled and seeded	4
¼ cup	red onion, diced	60 mL
¼ cup	red pepper, diced	60 mL
¼ cup	cucumber, diced	60 mL
I Tbsp.	balsamic vinegar	15 mL
I tsp.	garlic, minced	5 mL
½ tsp.	cayenne pepper	2 mL
I bunch	fresh cilantro	I bunch
pinch	salt and pepper	pinch
4 7-oz.	tuna loins	4 200-g

Preheat the barbecue (or heat up a frying pan).

To make the salsa, purée the tomatoes in a food processor. Combine the onion, red pepper, cucumber, vinegar, garlic, cayenne and cilantro in a bowl with the puréed tomatoes. Season.

Grill the tuna to rare on the barbecue (or sear it in a very hot frying pan). As it cooks, you will see it turning opaque from the bottom. Turn it over and continue cooking, but don't let it turn opaque all the way through. There should still be a red stripe around the middle. The cooking time depends on the thickness—about 5 minutes in total per inch (2.5 cm).

Place the tuna on plates with some salsa.

Wine suggestion
A Chardonnay or Sauvignon Blanc from New Zealand

Tandoori halibut cheeks

::

*Halibut cheeks are much like skate in texture, so be careful not to overcook them. The marinade helps
to keep the cheeks moist and tenderizes them somewhat as well. Halibut cheeks aren't available
all the time, but you can substitute halibut steaks or sea bass. Serve with Cinnamon Basmati Rice (page 119)
and either Sun-Dried Tomato Chutney (page 58) or Rhubarb Compote (page 44).
You may want to garnish the plates with fresh figs or roasted tomatoes.*

SERVES 4

2 cups	yogurt	500 mL
I Tbsp.	ground cumin seeds	15 mL
½ tsp.	cayenne pepper	2 mL
2 Tbsp.	coriander seeds, toasted	30 mL
I	garlic clove, minced	I
I Tbsp.	ginger, peeled and grated	15 mL
2 Tbsp.	fresh lemon juice	30 mL
I tsp.	salt	5 mL
3 Tbsp.	fresh cilantro, chopped	45 mL
1¾ lbs.	halibut cheeks	800 g

In a large bowl, mix together all the ingredients—except
the halibut. Cover the bowl and let sit in the refrigerator
for at least 1 hour, preferably overnight.

Place the halibut in the yogurt mixture and marinate in
the refrigerator for 2 to 6 hours.

Preheat the oven to 375°F (190°C).

Remove the halibut from the marinade, but let some of it
remain on the fish. Put the halibut on a baking sheet or in
a pan and roast in the oven for about 15 minutes until
done.

Cover the centre of each plate with the basmati rice and
top with the halibut cheeks. Place three dollops of chutney (or compote) around the edge of the rice.

Wine suggestion
A spicy Gewürztraminer

Smoked Alaska black cod
with sun-dried pepper sabayon

::

Sabayon is usually sweet, but here we make it savoury to create a cloud-light sauce for a rich fish. We also serve this sabayon with grilled salmon.

The recipe for the pepper purée will make more than is needed, but it keeps well for a week in a tightly covered jar in the fridge. To make Red Pepper mayonaise, mix the purée with mayonnaise, to taste, and serve it with Crabcakes (page 58).

SERVES 4

RED PEPPER PURÉE

	vegetable oil	
½ cup	red onion, diced	125 mL
I	garlic clove, minced	I
½ cup	sun-dried sweet red peppers	125 mL
½ cup	water	125 mL
I cup	white wine	250 mL

To make the red pepper purée, heat a small amount of vegetable oil in a frying pan, then sauté the onion and garlic until tender. Add the sun-dried red peppers, water and white wine. Cover the pot with a lid and simmer for 30 minutes.

Purée in a food processor until smooth. Strain to remove any seeds.

SABAYON

2	egg yolks	2
I Tbsp.	fresh lemon juice	15 mL
pinch	salt	pinch
½ cup	butter, softened	125 mL
drop	Worcestershire sauce	drop
drop	Tabasco sauce	drop
	salt and pepper	

To make the sabayon, place ¼ cup (50 mL) of the red pepper purée in a stainless steel bowl over simmering water (or the top of a double boiler), together with the egg yolks, lemon juice and salt. Whisk until the mixture is hot, fluffy and slightly thickened.

Whisk in the butter 1 Tbsp. (15 mL) at a time, until it is all incorporated. Add the Worcestershire and Tabasco, then season. Keep the sabayon at room temperature while you prepare the cod.

Roast ling cod
with garlic mashed potatoes

∷

*This dish is very simple and can be served
with many of the sauces in the book,
especially the Arugula Pesto (page 33). We serve it with
Garlic Mashed Potatoes (page 120).*

SERVES 4

4 7-oz.	smoked Alaska black cod fillets	4 200-g
2 tsp.	cracked black pepper	10 mL
4	baby leeks OR green onions, trimmed to 6 inches (15 cm)	4

To cook the cod, place the fillets in a shallow pan with
enough water to half cover the fish. Sprinkle each piece of
cod with ½ tsp. (2 mL) of the cracked black pepper and
cover the pan with a lid.

Bring the cod to a boil and simmer over medium-low heat
for 5 to 8 minutes until cooked through. Add the baby
leeks (or green onions) and steam lightly for 30 seconds.
Remove the pan from the heat.

To serve, cover the plates with the sabayon. Lift the fish
out of the cooking liquid with a slotted spatula and blot
on paper towels so that it won't discolour the sauce. Place
the fish on the sauce and garnish with a leek (or green
onion).

Wine suggestion
A buttery Chardonnay

4 7-oz.	ling cod fillets	4 200-g
pinch	sea salt	pinch
pinch	freshly ground black pepper	pinch
	vegetable oil	
4 Tbsp.	extra virgin olive oil	60 mL

Preheat the oven to 400°F (200°C).

Season the ling cod fillets with the sea salt and freshly
ground black pepper. Add a small amount of vegetable oil
to an ovenproof nonstick pan or cast-iron frying pan over
medium-high heat and sear the fillets on both sides.

Arrange the fillets skin-side down in the pan and roast in
the oven for 5 to 10 minutes (depending on the thickness
of the fish) until done.

To serve, set a mound of garlic mashed potatoes in the
centre of each plate and place the fish on top. Drizzle
1 Tbsp. (15 mL) of the olive oil over each fillet.

Wine suggestion
A Sauvignon Blanc from Washington state

Steamed sablefish
with lobster and vanilla bean sauce

::

Sablefish is also called butterfish because its cooked texture is silky, delicate and buttery.
This fish is very popular when smoked and is sold under the name of smoked Alaska black cod.

You don't need lobster meat for the sauce. Save the shells from a lobster meal to make the lobster stock
for the sauce, or ask a fishmonger to sell you the shells separately. Freeze any leftover sauce.

Vanilla bean works in either sweet or savoury applications.
In this recipe, we use vanilla as a spice, and it teams deliciously with the lobster.

SERVES 4

LOBSTER STOCK

8 oz.	lobster shells	250 g
2 cups	carrots, diced	500 mL
2 cups	leeks, diced	500 mL
1 cup	celery, diced	250 mL
2 cups	onions, diced	500 mL
8 cups	cold water	2 L
8	whole black peppercorns	8
¾ cup	lemongrass, chopped	180 mL

LOBSTER AND VANILLA BEAN SAUCE

2 Tbsp.	butter	30 mL
3 Tbsp.	flour	45 mL
1 cup	white wine	250 mL
1 cup	tomato sauce (page 150) OR puréed tomato	250 mL
2	vanilla beans	2
1 tsp.	salt	5 mL
½ cup	whipping cream	125 mL
	salt and pepper	

Preheat the oven to 400°F (200°C).

To make the stock, place the lobster shells in a pan and roast in the oven for 10 minutes. Add the vegetables and roast for another 10 minutes.

Place the lobster shells and vegetables in a large stockpot. Crush the shells with a meat hammer or a wooden spoon. Add the cold water, peppercorns and lemongrass. Bring to a boil and simmer for 30 minutes. Strain the stock through a sieve.

To make the sauce, place a soup pot over medium heat and melt the butter in it. Add the flour and whisk together to a make a roux. Stir in the white wine, 5 cups (1.25 L) lobster stock and tomato sauce (or puréed tomato).

Split the vanilla beans in half lengthwise and scrape out the seeds. Add the vanilla bean husks and seeds to the sauce. Add the salt and the whipping cream. Simmer for 30 minutes. Strain through a fine sieve and season.

4 7-oz.	sablefish fillets	4 200-g
3 Tbsp.	melted butter	45 mL
	salt and pepper	

Set up a steamer to cook the fish. At Bishop's, we use a Chinese bamboo steamer placed over a pot of boiling water. It is inexpensive and works very well.

Place a piece of parchment or wax paper under the fillets of fish in the steamer. This helps prevent sticking when removing the cooked fish.

Steam the sablefish for 4 to 6 minutes—the flesh will start to flake when done. Brush with the melted butter and season.

To serve, pour ¼ cup (60 mL) of the sauce on each place and arrange the fish on top.

Wine suggestion
An oaky Chardonnay from North America

Roast rack of lamb with fresh basil breadcrumbs

Seared loin of lamb with white beans, basil and red vermouth

Veal osso buco with burnt orange and Campari

Grilled flank steak with crisp summer greens

Shiitake-stuffed pork tenderloin with buttermilk dumplings

Roast pork chops with pear and green peppercorns

Escalope of veal with prosciutto and balsamic butter lettuce

Braised rabbit with black beans, tomato and pancetta

Medallions of venison with savoury chocolate raisin sauce

Mint pesto-stuffed roast leg of lamb

Roast rack of lamb
with fresh basil breadcrumbs

::

This is probably our best-selling entrée. We started making it for a regular customer although it wasn't on the menu and were so pleased with the effect of the basil that we put it on the menu. If you prefer, you can substitute mint for the basil. We serve this dish with Mashed Potatoes (page 120) and Sautéed Spinach, Garlic, Summer Squash and Cherry Tomatoes (page 103).

SERVES 4

SAUCE

2 Tbsp.	butter	30 mL
½ cup	shallots, chopped fine	125 mL
2 tsp.	garlic, minced	10 mL
¼ cup	red wine vinegar	60 mL
½ cup	red vermouth	125 mL
½ cup	fresh basil, chopped	125 mL
2 cups	veal demi-glace (page 149)	500 mL

To make the sauce, melt the butter in a saucepan, then sauté the shallots and garlic until tender. Add the vinegar and reduce until almost gone. Add the vermouth and basil, then reduce by half. Add the demi-glace and simmer for 30 minutes. Strain. (This sauce can be made a day in advance and will actually taste better after the flavour has developed for a day. Refrigerate until needed and reheat before serving.)

BASIL BREADCRUMBS

2 cups	fresh white bread, crusts removed and cubed	500 mL
½ cup	fresh basil, chopped	125 mL

To prepare the breadcrumbs, grind the fresh cubed bread in a food processor, until the crumbs are coarse. Add the basil and process until the crumbs are fine. If the mixture seems a little damp, spread it out on a baking sheet to dry out a bit.

	sea salt and freshly ground pepper	
2 2-lbs.	racks of lamb	2 1-kg
2 Tbsp.	Dijon mustard	30 mL

Preheat the oven to 400°F (200°F).

Heat up a frying pan. Season the lamb and sear in the frying pan on all sides. Transfer to a pan and roast in the oven until done—15 to 20 minutes for medium rare (depending on the size of the racks of lamb).

Five minutes before the lamb is done, remove it from the oven. Smear each rack with the mustard and sprinkle with the breadcrumbs, then return to the oven to lightly toast the crust. Remove from the oven and allow to rest for 10 minutes before carving.

To serve, reheat the sauce. Arrange the slices of lamb on plates with the mashed potatoes, vegetables and sauce.

Wine suggestion
A mature, full-bodied Cabernet or Merlot

Seared loin of lamb
with white beans, basil and red vermouth

::

This dish uses the eye of the rack of lamb instead of the thin, flat loins. After boning the lamb ribs, we use them for stock or barbecue them with a Szechuan sauce for a tasty sparerib dish.

SERVES 4

WHITE BEANS, BASIL AND RED VERMOUTH

1 cup	white beans	250 mL
2 cups	water	500 mL
2 Tbsp.	olive oil	30 mL
½ cup	onion, diced	125 mL
1 tsp.	garlic, minced	5 mL
¼ cup	fresh basil, chopped	60 mL
1 cup	red vermouth	250 mL
2 cups	chicken stock (page 146)	500 mL
½ cup	veal demi-glace (page 149)	125 mL
	salt and pepper	

	sea salt and freshly ground pepper	
1½ lbs.	boneless lamb loins	750 g
2 Tbsp.	Dijon mustard	30 mL
2 Tbsp.	fresh thyme leaves, chopped	30 mL

To prepare the beans, place them in a bowl with the water and soak overnight. Drain.

In a saucepan, heat the olive oil, then sauté the onion and garlic until tender. Add the basil, vermouth and beans. Simmer for 5 minutes. Add the stock and demi-glace, then season. (Season all bean and grain dishes as soon as the liquid is added, so the salt can penetrate the beans as they cook.)

Simmer the beans over medium-low heat for about 1½ hours until tender. Keep warm.

Preheat the oven to 400°F (200°F).

Place a cast-iron frying pan over medium heat. Season the lamb loins and sear on all sides. Place the pan in the oven and roast the lamb for 7 to 10 minutes, depending on its thickness, until desired doneness.

Take the lamb out of the oven. Smear with the Dijon mustard and sprinkle with the thyme leaves. Remove the meat from the pan and allow to rest for 5 minutes.

Spoon the beans onto plates. Slice the lamb loins and place them on top of the beans.

Wine suggestion
A red Spanish Rioja (a vanilla, soft, oaky wine)

Veal osso buco
with burnt orange and Campari

::

The meat and demi-glace are quite sweet, along with the caramelized orange and root vegetables.
In contrast, the Campari adds an intriguing note of bitterness.
Don't undercook the osso buco. The meat should fall off the bone.
It's even better the next day—just cover it with foil and reheat.

SERVES 4

4 lbs.	veal shanks, cut into pieces 1½ inches (4 cm) thick	1.8 kg
1	orange	1
1 cup	red onions, finely diced	250 mL
1 cup	carrots, finely diced	250 mL
1 cup	celery root, peeled and diced	250 mL
4	garlic cloves	4
2 Tbsp.	fresh rosemary leaves	30 mL
3½ oz.	Campari	100 mL
2 cups	veal demi-glace (page 149)	500 mL
1 cup	chicken stock (page 146)	250 mL

Preheat the oven to 350°F (180°C).

Use a sharp knife to score the outside of the veal shanks, to help stop the meat from curling up while cooking.

Place the shanks in a large pot and cover them with cold water. Bring to a boil and simmer for 30 minutes. Skim off any scum that rises to the surface. Remove the shanks from the water and arrange in a roasting pan.

Slice the orange and sear in a hot frying pan, until golden in colour.

Cover the blanched shanks with the orange slices, diced vegetables, garlic and rosemary. Pour the Campari over top.

In a saucepan, combine the demi-glace and chicken stock and bring to a boil. Pour over the shanks.

Cover the roasting pan with foil and place in the oven for 80 minutes.

To serve, place the veal shanks and sauce in large soup plates or bowls.

Wine suggestion
A rich, soft Brunello di Montalcino

Grilled flank steak
with crisp summer greens

::

Flank steak is a secondary cut of meat that's often overlooked because it is tough, though it has a rich flavour. The secret to making this cut tender is to buy well-aged meat. A few days in the oil marinade (make sure the steak is fully covered) ages it further. For this dish, you need crisp, solid greens that will stand up to the creamy dressing and the heat of the steak. We use arugula and romaine.

SERVES 4

MARINADE

2 cups	vegetable oil	500 mL
¼ cup	fresh thyme, chopped	60 mL
1 Tbsp.	freshly ground black pepper	15 mL
1 Tbsp.	paprika	15 mL
2 lbs.	flank steak	1 kg

To prepare the marinade, combine the oil, thyme, pepper and paprika in a large bowl. Add the flank steak and marinate in the refrigerator overnight or up to 3 days, making sure the meat is covered.

SALAD

1	egg	1
½ tsp	Dijon mustard	2 mL
2 Tbsp.	tarragon vinegar	30 mL
1 cup	vegetable oil	250 mL
¼ cup	light cream (half-and-half)	60 mL
2 Tbsp.	fresh parsley, chopped	30 mL
1 Tbsp.	fresh thyme, chopped	15 mL
1 Tbsp.	fresh rosemary, chopped	15 mL
	sea salt and pepper	
4 cups	salad greens, washed	1 L

To prepare the salad dressing, combine the egg, mustard and vinegar in a food processor. With the motor running, slowly add the oil in a small steady stream until incorporated. Add the light cream and herbs, then adjust the seasoning. Set aside.

Preheat the barbecue.

To cook the steak, first wipe off the excess marinade from the meat and season with sea salt. Grill for 5 to 7 minutes, until rare to medium rare. Do not cook the steak any more than medium rare, or it will become tough. Allow to rest 5 minutes before carving.

In a large bowl, toss the greens with the dressing, then mound the salad on plates. Slice the flank steak thinly across the grain and arrange on top of the greens.

Wine suggestion
A young red Burgundy

Shiitake-stuffed pork tenderloin
with buttermilk dumplings

::

We've tweaked the idea of duxelles (a stuffing with mushrooms) by using shiitake mushrooms and adding the extra flavour element of prunes. This recipe looks more complicated than it is. It consists of four parts: sauce, stuffing, dumplings and meat.

SERVES 4

SAUCE

2 Tbsp.	butter	30 mL
½ cup	shallots, chopped fine	125 mL
2 tsp.	garlic, minced	10 mL
¼ cup	celery root, peeled and chopped	60 mL
¼ cup	red wine vinegar	60 mL
4 oz.	port	125 mL
¼ cup	fresh thyme, chopped	60 mL
¼ cup	fresh rosemary, chopped	60 mL
2 cups	veal demi-glace (page 149)	500 mL

To prepare the sauce, melt the butter in a frying pan and sauté the shallots, garlic and celery root. Add the vinegar and reduce until almost gone. Add the port, thyme and rosemary, then reduce by half. Add the demi-glace and simmer for 30 minutes. Strain. (This sauce can be made a day in advance and will taste better after the flavour has developed for a day. Refrigerate until needed and reheat before serving.)

STUFFING

2 Tbsp.	butter	30 mL
½ cup	onion, diced	125 mL
1 tsp.	garlic, minced	5 mL
1 cup	shiitake mushrooms, stems removed and sliced	250 mL
½ cup	prunes, pitted and chopped	125 mL
2 Tbsp.	fresh rosemary	30 mL
½ cup	breadcrumbs	125 mL

To prepare the stuffing, melt the butter in a frying pan, then sauté the onion, garlic and mushrooms until tender. Add the prunes, rosemary and breadcrumbs. Transfer to a food processor and mix until well combined but not totally smooth.

BUTTERMILK DUMPLINGS

2 cups	potato, cooked and riced	500 mL
I cup	flour	250 mL
½ cup	buttermilk	125 mL
2	egg yolks	2
I cup	fresh breadcrumbs	250 mL
2 Tbsp.	fresh parsley, chopped	30 mL
I tsp.	salt	5 mL
4 cups	chicken stock (page xx)	I L

To prepare the dumpling dough, combine the potato, flour, buttermilk, egg yolks, breadcrumbs, parsley and salt in a food processor until well mixed. Allow to rest for 15 minutes.

To cook the dumplings, bring the chicken stock to a simmer. Roll the dough into small egg-shaped cylinders and poach in the chicken stock. If the dough seems too soft to shape, add a small amount of flour and roll the dumplings in flour before poaching them.

When the dumplings rise to the top, they are done. Remove with a slotted spoon and place them on a tray until the pork is ready.

I ½ lbs.	pork tenderloin	750 g
	vegetable oil	
	sea salt and freshly ground pepper	

Preheat the oven to 400°F (200°F).

Prepare the pork while the dumplings are cooking. Make an incision through the centre of the meat lengthwise, then pipe the stuffing into it. Rub the outside of the pork with vegetable oil and season.

Place the pork in a pan and roast in the oven for 20 minutes, or until slightly pink in the centre. Remove from the oven and allow to rest for 5 minutes before carving.

To serve, reheat the sauce. Reheat the dumplings in simmering chicken stock. Slice the pork and arrange on plates with the dumplings and sauce.

Wine suggestion
A Pinot Noir from Oregon state

Roast pork chops
with pear and green peppercorns

::

*To intensify the flavour of all spices and seeds, toast them
in a hot pan until you begin to smell them. When you toast the green peppercorns,
your kitchen will be filled with the seductive aroma of pepper.*

SERVES 4

THYME GLACE		
I tsp.	brine-packed green peppercorns	5 mL
I Tbsp.	butter	15 mL
4	garlic cloves, minced	4
I	onion, chopped	I
6 sprigs	fresh thyme	6 sprigs
2	cornichons, chopped	2
	salt and pepper	
I cup	Madeira	250 mL
2 cups	veal demi-glace (page 149)	500 mL

To make the thyme glace, toast the brine-packed pepper-corns in a hot frying pan until just fragrant.

Melt the butter in a frying pan and sauté the garlic, onion, thyme, cornichons and toasted green peppercorns until tender. Season, then deglaze the pan with the Madeira.

Add the veal demi-glace to the onion mixture and simmer for 30 minutes. Pass the glace through a sieve.

3 Tbsp.	clarified butter	45 mL
4	large pork chops	4
pinch	salt and pepper	pinch
I	ripe pear, sliced	I
I Tbsp.	brine-packed green peppercorns	15 mL

Preheat the oven to 350°F (180°F).

To prepare the pork chops, heat a medium saucepan and melt the clarified butter, then brown the pork chops on each side.

Season the pork chops, place them in a pan and roast in the oven for 5 to 6 minutes for every ½ inch (1.2 cm) of thickness.

To serve, reheat the glace. Arrange the pork chops on plates with the glace. Garnish with slices of ripe pear and brine-packed green peppercorns.

Wine suggestion
A Cabernet Sauvignon from California

Escalope of veal
with prosciutto and balsamic butter lettuce

∷

*Saltimbocca by any other name . . . The prosciutto should be sliced so thinly that you can
see the sage leaf through it; that way, the prosciutto will adhere to the veal.
If you make the sauce the day before, you can prepare this dish in just a few minutes.*

SERVES 4

SAUCE

2 Tbsp.	butter	30 mL
I	shallot, chopped fine	I
2 tsp.	garlic, minced	10 mL
¼ cup	balsamic vinegar	60 mL
½ cup	red wine	125 mL
¼ cup	fresh thyme, chopped	60 mL
¼ cup	fresh sage, chopped	60 mL
2 cups	veal demi-glace (page 149)	500 mL

To prepare the sauce, melt the butter in a saucepan, then
sauté the shallot and garlic until tender. Add the vinegar
and reduce until almost gone. Add the wine and herbs and
reduce by half. Add the demi-glace and simmer for 30
minutes. Strain. (This sauce can be made a day in advance
and will taste better after the flavour has developed for a
day. Refrigerate until needed.)

VEAL

4 7-oz.	veal escalopes	4 200-g
	freshly ground black pepper	
8	fresh sage leaves	8
4 slices	prosciutto	4 slices
	flour for dredging	
	vegetable oil	

To prepare the veal, season, then top each piece with two
sage leaves and a slice of prosciutto, pressing together lightly.

Dredge the veal in flour. Sauté quickly in a hot frying pan
with a small amount of vegetable oil for 2 to 3 minutes,
until still slightly pink.

Remove the meat from the pan and set aside. Add the
sauce to the pan and stir to deglaze. Keep warm.

SALAD

¼ cup	balsamic vinegar	60 mL
¾ cup	olive oil	180 mL
	salt and pepper	
2 heads	butter lettuce	2 heads

To prepare the vinaigrette, whisk together the vinegar and
olive oil in a small bowl. Season to taste.

Wash and drain the butter lettuce. In a large bowl, toss the
lettuce leaves with the vinaigrette.

To serve, arrange the lettuce leaves on plates. Place the veal
on the lettuce and drizzle the sauce over top.

Wine suggestion
*A good-quality red wine from Portugal or a light Pinot
Grigio or other floral from Italy, but not a dead-dry white
wine*

Braised rabbit
with black beans, tomato and pancetta

::

Michael Allemeier created this dish for a staff meal when we had the front legs left over from a rabbit special. It was a hit and went on the next menu. The Chinese fermented black beans are more a flavouring agent than a vegetable. They are available at most Asian food stores. Do not substitute regular black beans.

SERVES 4

2 Tbsp.	Chinese fermented black beans	30 mL
1	rabbit,	1
2-2½ lbs.	cut into pieces	1-1.3 kg
¼ cup	flour, for dredging	60 mL
1 tsp.	butter	5 mL
1 tsp.	ground coriander seeds	5 mL
1 tsp.	ground fennel seeds	5 mL
2 oz.	pancetta, sliced	60 g
½ cup	onion, sliced	125 mL
4	garlic cloves, minced	4
⅓ cup	Marsala	75 mL
3	medium-size tomatoes, chopped	3
1 cup	tomato sauce (page 150)	250 mL

Preheat the oven to 350°F (180°C).

Rinse the black beans well, as they are preserved in salt. Crush thoroughly.

Dredge the rabbit pieces in flour. In a soup pot, melt the butter and brown the rabbit pieces. Add the black beans, coriander, fennel, pancetta, onion and garlic. Sauté for 5 minutes.

Deglaze the pot with the Marsala. Stir in the tomatoes and tomato sauce. Transfer to a roasting pan and bake in the oven for 1 hour.

Wine suggestion
A red wine from Provence

Medallions of venison
with savoury chocolate raisin sauce

::

Tuscan hunters used to make this dish using wild boar,
and Michael Allemeier learned the recipe when he worked at a Tuscan restaurant. To buy venison,
ask your local butcher. If you can't find it there, try a German butcher.

SERVES 4

1 cup	vegetable oil	250 mL
2 Tbsp.	fresh rosemary	30 mL
1 1/2 lbs.	venison leg cutlets	750 g

Combine the oil and rosemary in a bowl. Add the venison and marinate it overnight in the refrigerator.

SAUCE

2 Tbsp.	butter	30 mL
1/2 cup	shallots, chopped fine	125 mL
2 tsp.	garlic, minced	10 mL
1/4 cup	balsamic vinegar	60 mL
1/2 cup	red wine	125 mL
1/4 cup	fresh rosemary, chopped	60 mL
2 cups	veal demi-glace (page 149)	500 mL

To prepare the sauce, melt the butter in a saucepan, then sauté the shallots and garlic until tender. Add the vinegar and reduce until almost gone. Add the red wine and rosemary, then reduce by half. Add the demi-glace and simmer for 30 minutes. Strain. (This sauce can be made a day in advance and will taste better after the flavour has developed for a day. Refrigerate until needed.)

1/4 cup	raisins	60 mL
1/4 cup	white wine	60 mL
2 Tbsp.	cocoa powder	30 mL
1/4 cup	warm water	60 mL
	sea salt and freshly ground pepper	
	vegetable oil	

In a small bowl, soak the raisins in the white wine for 2 to 3 hours, until swollen and puffy.

In another bowl, mix the cocoa with the warm water until very smooth. To prevent lumping, add the water a little bit at a time.

Remove the venison from the marinade and wipe off the excess oil. Season. Heat a small amount of vegetable oil in a heavy frying pan, then sear the venison for 1 to 2 minutes on each side, until browned but still quite rare. (Venison cooked more than medium will be tough.)

Remove the venison from the pan and place on plates.

Add the raisins and white wine to the pan, stirring to deglaze. Add the cocoa mixture, whisking until smooth, then add the sauce. Simmer until hot. Spoon the sauce over the venison and serve.

Wine suggestion
A Merlot from Washington state

Mint pesto–stuffed roast leg of lamb

::

Peppermint, spearmint and English mint are the best varieties for this dish.
You want an assertive mint flavour. The parsley tones it down somewhat and imparts a bright green colour.

Ask your butcher to debone the leg of lamb for you, or buy a boneless leg.

SERVES 4

MINT PESTO

1 cup	fresh mint leaves	250 mL
1	garlic clove	1
½ cup	pine nuts, toasted	125 mL
½ cup	fresh parsley	125 mL
½ tsp.	salt	2 mL
½ cup	olive oil	125 mL

To prepare the mint pesto, place the mint, garlic, pine nuts and parsley in a food processor, then grind into a paste. Add the salt. With the motor running, slowly add the olive oil.

1 3-4 lbs.	leg of lamb, boneless	1 1.4-1.8 kg
¼ cup	olive oil	60 mL
	salt and pepper	

Preheat the oven to 350°F (180°C).

Open the leg of lamb and spread the mint pesto into all the cracks. Reassemble the leg and use butcher's twine to tie it back together.

Brush the leg with the olive oil and season well. Place in a pan and roast in the oven to the desired doneness, about 12 minutes per pound (450 g) for pink lamb. Let rest for 15 minutes in a warm place. Carve into very thin slices.

Wine suggestion
A Châteauneuf-du-Pape or any other Côtes-du-Rhône red

Roast chicken breast with wild mushroom risotto and sage pan gravy

Whole roast chicken with cornbread stuffing and chipotle sauce

Roast duck breast with berries and ginger

Lacquered duck legs with mashed potatoes

Tandoori chicken breast with fruit chutney

Roast quail stuffed with pine nuts, cherries and spinach

Roast chicken breast
with wild mushroom risotto and sage pan gravy

∷

One of the biggest hits we've ever had, this dish has been on our past two fall menus.
We cook the chicken breast on the bone for more flavour.

Making risotto is an art: it takes about 30 minutes to cook, and you have to pay close attention.
Arborio rice is the only kind to use to achieve the creamy but firm texture.

SERVES 4

WILD MUSHROOM RISOTTO		
2 Tbsp.	butter	30 mL
I cup	onions, diced	250 mL
I tsp.	garlic, minced	5 mL
¼ cup	fresh sage, chopped	60 mL
2 cups	wild mushrooms, sliced	500 mL
2 cups	arborio rice	500 mL
	salt and pepper	
½ cup	white wine	125 mL
4 cups	chicken stock (page 146)	I L
I cup	heavy cream	250 mL
¼ cup	Parmesan cheese, grated	60 mL

To prepare the risotto, melt the butter in a wide shallow pan and sweat the onions, garlic and sage until almost clear. Add the mushrooms and sauté until lightly coloured. Add the rice and sauté until the grains are slightly transparent. Season.

Deglaze the pan with the white wine. Add enough chicken stock to cover the rice by ½ inch (1.2 cm) and simmer. Stir frequently, adding stock to keep the rice covered, allowing that to be absorbed, then adding more as needed.

When the rice is 90 per cent cooked, add the heavy cream and Parmesan, then continue cooking and stirring until the rice is still creamy but thick enough to mound slightly on the plate.

	sea salt and freshly ground pepper	
4	chicken breast halves, bone in	4
¼ cup	flour, for dredging	60 mL
	vegetable oil	

While the risotto is simmering, preheat the oven to 400°F (200°C).

Season the chicken breasts and dredge them in flour, shaking off the excess.

Heat a small amount of vegetable oil in a cast-iron frying pan and sear the chicken until lightly browned. Place the pan in the oven and roast for 25 minutes.

Remove the chicken to a platter and allow to rest for 10 minutes. Reserve the pan juices.

SAGE PAN GRAVY

	flour	
¼ cup	dry sherry	60 mL
2 Tbsp.	fresh sage, chopped	30 mL
I cup	chicken stock (page 146)	250 mL

To make the gravy, sprinkle a small amount of flour into the pan juices and cook over medium heat, whisking to form a paste. Add the sherry and sage, stirring until incorporated.

Add the chicken stock, stirring until the gravy is well blended and free of lumps. Simmer for 5 minutes to thicken slightly, then strain.

To serve, debone the chicken breasts. Mound the risotto on plates and place a chicken breast on top. Drizzle the gravy around the outside.

Wine suggestion
A Valpolicella or a Pinot Grigio

Whole roast chicken
with cornbread stuffing and chipotle sauce

::

*One of our original ideas when Bishop's was conceived was to have a restaurant
where people could order a whole roast chicken, served family-style.
Well, the concept did change somewhat, but here's a whole roast chicken that you can serve family-style.*

A chipotle is a dried, smoked jalapeño pepper.

SERVES 4

CORNBREAD STUFFING

2 Tbsp.	olive oil	30 mL
½ cup	red onion, diced	125 mL
½ cup	celery, diced	125 mL
¾ cup	pearl onions, peeled	185 mL
4 cups	day-old cornbread, crumbled (page 142)	1 L
¼ cup	fresh cilantro, coarsely chopped	60 mL
¼ cup	fresh parsley, coarsely chopped	60 mL
	salt and pepper	
1	roasting chicken	1
4-5 lbs.		1.8-2.3 kg
	sea salt and freshly ground pepper	

Preheat the oven to 400°F (200°C).

To prepare the stuffing, heat the olive oil in a frying pan and sauté the red onion, celery and pearl onions until golden. Place in a large bowl and toss with the cornbread, cilantro and parsley. Season.

Spoon the stuffing into the chicken. Rub the skin of the chicken with sea salt and pepper. Place in a roasting pan and cook in the oven for 20 minutes per pound (450 g), or until the juice from the thigh runs clear when pierced with a fork. Remove from the oven and allow to rest for 15 minutes before carving.

CHIPOTLE SAUCE

2 Tbsp.	olive oil	30 mL
½ cup	fennel bulb, sliced	125 mL
½ cup	red onion, diced	125 mL
1 tsp.	garlic, minced	5 mL
1	chipotle	1
½ cup	white wine	125 mL
2 cups	tomatoes, chopped	500 mL

While the chicken is roasting, prepare the sauce. Heat the olive oil in a saucepan and sauté the fennel, red onion and garlic until soft. Add the chipotle, white wine and tomatoes.

Simmer the sauce for 30 minutes over medium-low heat. Pass through a food mill with a coarse blade and return to the pan. Keep warm until needed.

To serve, carve the chicken. Pour the sauce on the plates and place the chicken on top of the sauce, with some stuffing at the side.

Wine suggestion
A light young Zinfandel

>
Whole roast chicken with cornbread stuffing and chipotle sauce

Roast duck breast
with berries and ginger

::

If you can find fresh duck (frozen duck can be dry and tough), which still isn't easy, you'll find this a quick and simple recipe. Many people are reluctant to cook duck because of its reputation for being fatty, but this is a recipe for summer, when ducks are leaner. This recipe uses only the breasts—for the legs, see Lacquered Duck Legs with Mashed Potatoes (page 98).

SERVES 4

2	ducks	2
5-6 lbs.		2.3-2.7 kg
	sea salt and freshly ground pepper	
I tsp.	garlic, minced	5 mL
3 Tbsp.	ginger, peeled and chopped	45 mL
I Tbsp.	fresh thyme, chopped	15 mL
¼ cup	balsamic vinegar	60 mL
I cup	fresh berries (blackberries, blueberries, raspberries, black currants or a combination)	250 mL
½ cup	chicken stock (page 146)	125 mL

Preheat the oven to 425°F (220°C).

Remove the breasts, cut in half and debone. Prick the skin all over with a fork and season. Sear in a heavy ovenproof skillet over medium-high heat, 2 minutes per side. Pour off any fat.

Place the skillet in the oven (with the duck skin side up) and roast for 5 minutes. Remove the skillet from the oven, pour off any fat, turn the duck skin side down, then return to the oven for another 5 minutes (for medium rare). Remove from the oven and place the duck on a platter to rest.

Add the garlic, ginger and thyme to the skillet in which you cooked the duck and sauté until fragrant. Add the vinegar and reduce to 1 Tbsp. (15 mL). Add the berries and chicken stock, then reduce by half.

Slice the duck meat at an angle, arrange it on plates and spoon the sauce over top.

Wine suggestion
A Beaujolais or a Côte de Beaune red

<
Shiitake-stuffed
pork tenderloin
with buttermilk
dumplings, page 86

Lacquered duck legs
with mashed potatoes

::

If you made the Roast Duck Breast with Berries and Ginger (page 97), this recipe uses the legs.
The breast and legs have to be cooked separately because the cooking times and styles are so different.
For this dish, Michael Allemeier combined two traditional ways of serving duck—
Chinese lacquered duck and the technique of French confit. We serve it with Mashed Potatoes (page 120).

SERVES 4

I 2-inch	piece of ginger, peeled and finely chopped	I 5-cm
I head	garlic, finely chopped	I head
I cup	soy sauce	250 mL
3 cups	water	750 mL
4 Tbsp.	dried tarragon	60 mL
4 Tbsp.	coriander seeds, toasted	60 mL
½ cup	corn syrup	125 mL
½ cup	red wine vinegar	125 mL
4	duck legs, thigh boned out	4

In a large bowl, combine all the ingredients (except the duck legs) and whisk well. Add the duck legs and marinate in the refrigerator for 3 days.

Preheat the oven to 275°F (140°C),

Drain the duck legs, place them in a roasting pan and cook slowly in the oven for 1 hour. After that, turn up the oven heat to 325°F (160°C) for 30 minutes, then to 375°F (190°C) for an additional 30 minutes.

Let the duck cool for use later or serve at once with mashed potatoes.

To serve the duck legs later, reheat them in the oven at 300°F (150°C) for 15 minutes.

Wine suggestion
A Gewürztraminer from the Pacific Northwest

Tandoori chicken breast
with fruit chutney

::

*The best fruits for this chutney are mango, peach, apricot, apple and pear. Other types will work;
just make sure they are ripe. As well as varying the fresh fruit, we also vary the dried component—try dried
cranberries or cherries instead of raisins. Michael Allemeier calls this a fill-in-the-blanks chutney recipe.
Do not freeze leftover chutney. It will keep for 3 to 4 weeks in the refrigerator.*

We serve this dish with Cinnamon Basmati Rice (page 119).

SERVES 4

FRUIT CHUTNEY

I cup	sugar	250 mL
I ¼ cups	white wine vinegar	300 mL
3	garlic cloves	3
3 Tbsp.	ginger, peeled and grated	45 mL
I	jalapeño pepper	I
2 lbs.	fruit	I kg
½ cup	raisins	125 mL
I stick	cinnamon	I stick

Combine the sugar and vinegar in a large stainless steel
pot. Bring to a boil, stirring to dissolve the sugar.

In a food processor, combine the garlic, ginger and
jalapeño. Purée, adding a touch of vinegar to form a paste.
Add to the vinegar and sugar mixture and bring to a boil.

Add the fruit, raisins and cinnamon stick. Simmer for 20
to 30 minutes until the mixture thickens. Monitor the
temperature and watch to make sure the chutney doesn't
stick or burn on the bottom. Let cool. Makes 4 cups (1 L).

TANDOORI MARINADE

2 cups	yogurt	500 mL
I Tbsp.	ground cumin	15 mL
½ tsp.	cayenne pepper	2 mL
2 Tbsp.	coriander seeds, toasted	30 mL
I	garlic clove, minced	I
I Tbsp.	ginger, peeled and grated	15 mL
2 Tbsp.	lemon juice	30 mL
I Tbsp.	orange juice	15 mL
I tsp.	salt	5 mL
2 Tbsp.	fresh cilantro, chopped	30 mL
2 Tbsp.	fresh mint, chopped	30 mL
4 7-oz.	boneless chicken breast halves	4 200-g

Roast quail stuffed with pine nuts, cherries and spinach

::

The stuffing is a vegetable accent, rather than the usual starch-based one. Quail has a slightly gamey flavour that goes well with the earthiness of the spinach.

SERVES 4

In a bowl, mix together all the ingredients (except for the chicken). Add the chicken and marinate in the refrigerator for 6 hours or, preferably, overnight.

Preheat the oven to 375°F (190°C).

Remove the chicken from the marinade and place on a baking sheet or in a roasting pan. Roast in the oven for 30 to 35 minutes, until the chicken is done.

Serve the chicken with fruit chutney and rice.

Wine suggestion
A Champagne or a Spanish sparkling wine

STUFFING		
2 cups	spinach, blanched, wrung out and chopped	500 mL
¼ cup	pine nuts, toasted	60 mL
¼ cup	sun-dried cherries, chopped	60 mL
2	shallots, diced	2
2	garlic cloves, minced	2
I tsp.	ground nutmeg	5 mL
8	quails	8
¼ cup	clarified butter **OR** olive oil	60 mL
pinch	salt and pepper	pinch

Preheat the oven to 450°F (230°C).

To prepare the stuffing, thoroughly mix together the first six ingredients in a bowl. Spoon the stuffing into the quails.

Place the quails in a roasting pan and brush them with the clarified butter (or olive oil). Season. Roast in the oven for 15 minutes, basting every 5 minutes. When the birds turn golden brown, they're done. Serve at once.

Wine suggestion
A Cabernet (vino da tavola) from Tuscany

Sautéed spaghetti squash with garlic and peppers

Rosemary vegetable brochette

Sautéed spinach, garlic, summer squash and cherry tomatoes

Potato and rosemary strudel

Wild mushrooms sautéed with thyme, pears and green peppercorns

Vegetable coconut curry

Eggplant tart

Roasted eggplant stuffed with bocconcini

Vegetable hash with basil pesto

Squash ragoût with cumin lentils

Vegetarian pesto pizza

Sautéed spaghetti squash with garlic and peppers

::

We serve this as an accompaniment to our Pan-Seared Scallops with Lemongrass and Chervil Sauce (page 60). Cutting the spaghetti squash across the middle rather than lengthwise results in longer strands. Cut the squash as soon as it comes out of the oven and let it cool, so that the strands will hold together better.

SERVES 4

1 2-lbs.	spaghetti squash	1 1-kg
2 Tbsp.	butter	30 mL
1 cup	red pepper, diced	125 mL
½ cup	green pepper, diced	125 mL
1 tsp.	garlic, minced	5 mL
½ cup	zucchini, diced	125 mL
	salt and pepper	
2 Tbsp.	fresh chives, chopped	30 mL

Preheat the oven to 375°F (190°C).

Pierce the squash once with a knife to prevent it from bursting and bake it in the oven for 40 minutes. Remove the squash from the oven, cut in half and let cool. Remove the seeds and use a fork to flake the flesh into long strands.

In a frying pan, melt the butter and sauté the red and green peppers, garlic and zucchini until fragrant. Add the spaghetti squash and season. Cook over medium heat until heated through. Toss with the chives and serve.

Rosemary vegetable brochette

::

Dennis Green recommends using a cast-iron grill pan, the kind with a ridged surface, to do this kind of cooking indoors on top of the stove. This dish goes well with fish or meat.

SERVES 4 TO 8

8 sprigs	fresh rosemary, 8 inches (20 cm) long	8 sprigs
2 Tbsp.	olive oil	30 mL
1	orange, zest and juice	1
16	cherry tomatoes	16
1	red pepper, cut into 16 pieces	1
16	baby pattypan squash	16
16	shiitake mushrooms	16
	salt and pepper	

Trim the leaves off the rosemary sprigs, except for the top 2 inches (5 cm). Reserve the leaves. Cut the bottom of each sprig at an angle to form a point, to make it easier to skewer the vegetables.

To make the marinade, chop the trimmed rosemary leaves and combine them with the olive oil, orange zest and juice.

Skewer the cherry tomatoes, red pepper pieces, squash and mushrooms on the rosemary sprigs, two of each per brochette.

Brush the brochettes with the marinade and season. Grill for 5 to 8 minutes, turning occasionally, until the vegetables are tender.

Sautéed spinach, garlic, summer squash and cherry tomatoes

::

Zucchini, crookneck, pattypan or any summer squash will work in this dish. Buy the smallest ones you can—if you find baby squash, leave them whole. In the restaurant, we serve this to accompany rack of lamb. You can also serve it with fresh bread as a light lunch dish.

SERVES 4 OR 8

2 Tbsp.	butter	30 mL
1 Tbsp.	olive oil	15 mL
4 cups	summer squash (1 lb./500 g), sliced	1 L
1 Tbsp.	garlic, minced	15 mL
2 cups	cherry tomatoes	500 mL
8 cups	spinach leaves (8 oz./250 g)	2 L
	salt and pepper	

In a large frying pan, heat the butter and olive oil. Sauté the squash until it begins to colour. Add the garlic and tomatoes, then cook until the squash is almost done. Add the spinach and toss until the leaves wilt. Season and serve.

Potato and rosemary strudel

::

You can serve large portions of this strudel with a salad for a whole meal or serve smaller slices for a beautiful starch accompaniment to a main dish. Frozen puff pastry works fine.

SERVES 2 OR 4

1 Tbsp.	butter	15 mL
1	shallot, finely diced	1
1	garlic clove, minced	1
5 Tbsp.	sour cream	75 mL
1	egg yolk	1
1 Tbsp.	fresh rosemary leaves, chopped	15 mL
1	jumbo russet potato, cut into a rectangle—when sliced it should yield 1 cup (250 mL)	1
	freshly ground black pepper	
7 oz.	puff pastry	200 g
1	egg white	1
1 Tbsp.	coarse rock salt	15 mL

In a frying pan, melt the butter, then sauté the shallot and garlic until transparent.

In a bowl, combine the shallot mixture with the sour cream, egg yolk and rosemary.

Using a mandoline cutter or a very sharp knife, cut the potato into very thin slices (you should be able to see through them) and add to the sour cream mixture. Season with the black pepper.

Preheat the oven to 300°F (150°C).

Roll out the puff pastry into a rectangle 9 inches (23 cm) wide and 6 inches (15 cm) tall, with a thickness of ⅛ to ¼ inch (3 to 6 mm).

Spread the potato mixture down the centre third of the pastry, leaving a third clear on each side. Fold the left flap of pastry over the potatoes to cover them.

Using a pastry cutter or a sharp knife, cut horizontal lines in the right flap of pastry every ½ inch (1.2 cm). Brush the top of the folded-over pastry with half of the egg white. Fold the strips of pastry over the folded-over part to form a lattice, pressing lightly to make sure they adhere. Neatly secure all the end pieces under the strudel. Brush the top with the remaining egg white.

Place the strudel on a baking sheet and bake in the oven for 40 to 50 minutes, until the pastry is golden brown and the potato is cooked. Cut into slices 1¼ to 2 inches (3 to 5 cm) wide and serve at once.

Wild mushrooms
sautéed with thyme, pears and green peppercorns

::

Serve this with game or a roast.
It's a hearty winter dish, but still light.

SERVES 4

¼ cup	butter	60 mL
2	shallots, sliced	2
1 tsp.	garlic, minced	5 mL
1 tsp.	green peppercorns	5 mL
1 lb.	wild mushrooms, whole	500 g
1 tsp.	fresh thyme leaves	5 mL
1 cup	sherry OR port	250 mL
1 cup	chicken stock (page 146)	250 mL
2	pears	2
pinch	salt and pepper	pinch
	melba toast OR buttered toast	
	fresh thyme for garnish	

In a saucepan over medium heat, melt the butter and sauté the shallots, garlic and green peppercorns until tender.

Add the mushrooms and thyme, then sauté until tender. Deglaze the pan with the sherry (or port) and add the chicken stock.

Slice the pears (you don't have to peel them) and add them to the mushroom mixture. Continue to cook it until almost all of the liquid is gone. Season.

Serve in a bowl on melba toast (or buttered toast). Garnish with fresh thyme.

Vegetable coconut curry

::

Bishop's is no longer open for lunch, but this main dish was a popular lunch menu item for many years. The recipe makes quite a bit, but it just keeps getting better and better as it sits, so you can look forward to leftovers. Serve it with Cinnamon Basmati Rice (page 119). The coconut milk is readily available in cans.

SERVES 6

¼ cup	clarified butter	60 mL
I tsp.	coriander seeds	5 mL
I tsp.	fennel seeds	5 mL
I Tbsp.	curry powder	15 mL
I Tbsp.	ground cumin seeds	15 mL
4	cloves	4
2 sticks	cinnamon	2 sticks
I Tbsp.	garlic, minced	15 mL
2	onions, chopped	2
I cup	carrots, cubed	250 mL
I cup	turnip, cubed	250 mL
I cup	rutabaga, cubed	250 mL
I cup	cauliflower, florets	250 mL
I cup	zucchini, cubed	250 mL
I cup	red pepper, cubed	250 mL
I cup	celery, sliced	250 mL
4 cups	coconut milk	I L
2 cups	tomato sauce (page 150)	500 mL
	fresh cilantro sprigs for garnish	

In a large soup pot over medium heat, melt the clarified butter and sauté the coriander, fennel, curry powder, cumin, cloves, cinnamon and garlic.

Add the onions, carrots, turnip, rutabaga and cauliflower. Sauté for 20 minutes.

Add the zucchini, red pepper, celery, coconut milk and tomato sauce. Simmer for another 20 minutes.

Place a mound of basmati rice in each bowl and top with the curry. Garnish with a sprig of cilantro.

Eggplant tart

::

This tart resembles an elegant pizza and is good as a vegetable side dish, a starter or a light lunch, served with a salad. The flavour depends on the eggplant, so it's important to prepare it properly and to cook it slowly at low heat. Instead of the puff pastry, you can use 4 large vols-au-vent.

SERVES 4

I	eggplant	I
I ½ tsp.	salt	7 mL
I Tbsp.	olive oil	I5 mL
I	sheet of puff pastry	I
	(12 × 24 inches/30 × 60 cm)	
I	egg, beaten	I
I cup	tomato sauce (page I50)	250 mL
I Tbsp.	fresh basil, chopped	I5 mL
½ cup	fresh parsley, chopped	125 mL
4	tomatoes, sliced	4
½ cup	Parmesan cheese, grated	125 mL
	olive oil	

To prepare the eggplant, cut it lengthwise into slices ½ inch (1.2 cm) thick. Salt the slices and allow to drain for 20 to 30 minutes on paper towels. Brush on the olive oil. Grill, roast or sauté the eggplant for 6 to 7 minutes, until it is soft but not dried out.

Preheat the oven to 400°F (200°C).

Brush the sheet of puff pastry with the beaten egg. Fold the pastry in half lengthwise, then cut it into 4 rectangles. Place them on a baking sheet and bake in the oven for 12 to 14 minutes until golden.

Let the pastry cool and scoop out the centres, leaving a ⅛-inch (2-mm) border. Spoon ¼ cup (60 mL) of the tomato sauce into each piece of puff pastry. Sprinkle with the chopped basil and parsley.

Place 4 layers, alternating the tomato and eggplant, in each piece of puff pastry. Top with the grated Parmesan cheese and sprinkle with olive oil. Bake in the oven for 10 to 15 minutes, until the cheese melts.

Roasted eggplant
stuffed with bocconcini

::

This recipe calls for the long thin Japanese eggplants.
Get them small and heavy for their size.
Japanese eggplants don't require salting
like the Italian ones because they don't have
the same bitter taste.

SERVES 4

8	Japanese eggplants	8
I Tbsp.	olive oil	15 mL
pinch	salt and pepper	pinch
12 oz.	bocconcini, sliced	350 g
I Tbsp.	garlic, minced	15 mL
2 cups	tomato sauce (page 150)	500 mL
I Tbsp.	parsley, chopped	15 mL

Preheat the oven to 400°F (200°C).

Brush the eggplants with the olive oil and season. Prick with a fork and bake in the oven for 20 to 30 minutes until tender. Let cool and split lengthwise down the centre. Stuff with the bocconcini and garlic.

Cover the bottom of a baking pan with the tomato sauce. Place the eggplants on the tomato sauce and bake in the oven for 30 to 40 minutes, until the cheese melts.

Arrange on plates and garnish with the chopped parsley.

Vegetable hash
with basil pesto

::

For a traditional touch to this untraditional hash,
place a poached egg on top.
Good for breakfast, lunch or a side dish.

SERVES 4

3 Tbsp.	butter	45 mL
½ cup	red pepper, diced	125 mL
½ cup	red onion, diced	125 mL
½ cup	zucchini, diced	125 mL
½ cup	eggplant, diced	125 mL
¼ cup	sun-dried tomatoes, chopped	60 mL
¼ cup	sun-dried olives, chopped	60 mL
½ cup	basil pesto (page 151)	125 mL

Melt the butter in a saucepan and sauté all the vegetables until tender. Stir in the basil pesto and serve in bowls.

Squash ragoût with cumin lentils

::

Vegans love this dish as a main course.
The combination of summer and winter squash gives it different textures. Use summer squash
such as zucchini, pattypan or crookneck, and winter squash such as banana or butternut.

SERVES 4

CUMIN LENTILS

2 Tbsp.	butter	30 mL
2 Tbsp.	vegetable oil	30 mL
I cup	onions, diced	250 mL
2 Tbsp.	ground cumin seeds	30 mL
I Tbsp.	paprika	15 mL
I tsp.	curry powder	5 mL
2 tsp.	garlic, minced	10 mL
I ½ cups	Indian green lentils	375 mL
½ cup	white wine	125 mL
I tsp.	salt	5 mL
I tsp.	freshly ground pepper	5 mL
4 ½ cups	vegetable stock (page 148)	1.125 L
2 Tbsp.	parsley, chopped	30 mL

SQUASH RAGOÛT

I Tbsp.	butter	15 mL
I Tbsp.	olive oil	15 mL
4 cups	summer squash (I lb./500 g), sliced	I L
I cup	red onions, sliced	250 mL
2 tsp.	garlic, minced	10 mL
3 cups	winter squash (I lb./500 g), in I ½ inch (4 cm) cubes	750 mL
2 cups	tomatoes, diced	500 mL
I cup	vegetable stock (page 148)	250 mL
¼ cup	white wine	60 mL
¼ cup	fresh basil, chopped	60 mL
2 Tbsp	fresh thyme, chopped	60 mL
	salt and pepper	
¼ cup	green onions, chopped	60 mL

To prepare the lentils, heat the butter and oil in a large frying pan, then sauté the onions until clear. Add the cumin, paprika, curry powder and garlic, then cook until fragrant.

Add the lentils and sauté until well coated, so the flavour will penetrate. Add the wine and deglaze the pan, scraping all of the browned spices off the bottom.

Add the salt, pepper and vegetable stock. Reduce the heat to medium-low and simmer for 30 minutes, or until the lentils are tender. Add the parsley and keep warm.

To make the ragoût, heat the butter and oil in a large frying pan. Sauté the summer squash, red onions and garlic until they begin to colour.

Add the winter squash, tomatoes, vegetable stock and white wine. Add the basil and thyme, then season. Simmer for 5 to 10 minutes, until the squash is tender and the liquid is reduced.

To serve, ladle the lentils into shallow bowls and spoon the ragoût over top. Garnish with the green onions.

Vegetarian pesto pizza

::

A very popular dish.
Our pesto recipe doesn't have very much oil in it,
so it won't result in a sodden pizza. If you're
not a vegetarian, add some thinly sliced pancetta.

SERVES 4 TO 6

	olive oil	
½ cup	basil pesto (page 151)	125 mL
½ cup	tomato sauce (page 150)	125 mL
½ cup	red pepper, diced	125 mL
½ cup	zucchini, diced	125 mL
½ cup	onion, diced	125 mL
½ cup	tomato, sliced	125 mL
½ cup	mushrooms, sliced	125 mL
½ cup	Parmesan cheese, grated	125 mL

Preheat the oven to 350°F (180°C).

For the pizza shell, make half of the Focaccia recipe (page 141). Roll out to fit a 14-inch (35-cm) pizza pan.

Brush the pan with a little olive oil and place the pizza shell on it. Spread ¼ cup (60 mL) of the pesto over the pizza shell. Place the pan in the oven for 10 minutes to partially bake the pizza shell.

Spread the remaining basil pesto and the tomato sauce on the pizza shell. Arrange the vegetables on the tomato sauce, and sprinkle the Parmesan over top.

Bake the pizza in the oven for about 30 minutes, until the dough is cooked. Serve at once.

Ravioli stuffed with crab, mascarpone and eggplant

Spaetzle

Carrot and cilantro risotto

Spinach and basil cannelloni

Barley risotto with shiitake mushrooms

Chanterelle and Asiago lasagne

Pesto linguine with grilled eggplant and poached bocconcini

Cinnamon basmati rice

Horseradish griddle cakes

Mashed potatoes and variations:

Garlic / Sun-dried tomato and green onion

Crisp potato pancakes

Nugget potatoes stuffed with Pernod butter

Ravioli stuffed with
crab, mascarpone and eggplant

::

If you like to make your own pasta, you can make the cannelloni squares; otherwise, buy fresh ones ready made.
We have served this ravioli with a dab of a chunky roasted tomato sauce accented
with toasted coriander seeds, but many other sauces or condiments would also go well with it,
such as a white wine cream sauce, a Parmesan cheese sauce or a fresh herb sauce.

SERVES 4

2 Tbsp.	olive oil	60 mL
4	shallots, finely diced	4
2	garlic cloves, diced	2
2 cups	Japanese eggplant, cut into ½-inch (1-cm) cubes	500 mL
1 cup	mascarpone	250 mL
1 lb.	crabmeat	500 g
¼ cup	Parmesan cheese, grated	60 mL
	salt and pepper	
1 lb.	cannelloni sheets (5 × 6 inches / 12 × 16 cm)	500 g
1	egg	1

Add the olive oil to a frying pan over medium heat. Sauté the shallots, garlic and eggplant, until the eggplant is tender and golden.

Turn the heat down to low and add the mascarpone, slowly melting it in. Keep stirring the whole time to prevent the mascarpone from sticking.

When the mascarpone has all been melted, remove the pan from the heat and put the mixture into a bowl. Stir in the crabmeat and the Parmesan cheese, then season. Let cool.

Once the filling is cold to the touch, make up the ravioli. Cut the cannelloni sheets into 5 × 3 inch (12 × 8 cm) rectangles.

Whip the egg to make an egg wash.

Place 2 Tbsp. (30 mL) of filling on half of each pasta sheet. Brush the egg wash around the edges and fold the empty side over top of the filling, pressing down to seal well.

Bring a large pot of salted water to a boil. Carefully add the ravioli to the water and cook for 7 to 8 minutes, until they rise to the surface and float. Remove using a slotted spoon and serve.

Spaetzle

::

Spaetzle can be adapted either to match the main dish or to provide an interesting contrast,
and we come up with new ideas almost every day. Once, to accompany a duck dish,
we used reduced Merlot instead of the warm water in the recipe. At other times we have variously added
blanched wrung-out spinach with basil, turmeric, mustard, sage or tomato juice.

The metric measures for the spaetzle are more precise than those given in imperial.
To achieve the best results, try using the metric measures. Note that a couple of these are by weight, which is more
dependable and accurate than volume, so watch out for them and use a kitchen scale calibrated in metric.

SERVES 4

3½ cups	sifted flour	500 g
8	egg yolks	8
1½ cups	warm water	400 mL
½ cup	parsley, chopped	20 g
1½ tsp.	salt	7 mL

Add the flour and the yolks to a large bowl and use a wooden spoon to mix together until crumbly. Slowly add the warm water to make the dough. Add the parsley and salt. Let rest for 20 minutes.

Bring a large pot of salted water to a boil.

To cook the spaetzle, use a spaetzle press or hold a colander over the boiling water and push the dough through the holes. The dough will break into small chunks. If the pot is big enough, you can put all the spaetzle into the water; otherwise, cook in batches so they won't stick to each other.

When the spaetzle are done, they float. Remove and rinse in cold water. When cool to the touch, remove and drain well. Refrigerate until needed.

To serve, reheat the spaetzle by sautéing them in a frying pan with a little butter or olive oil until golden brown.

Carrot and cilantro risotto

::

When you cook risotto or any other dish that involves a long simmering process,
it's important to season the dish early in the cooking process to allow the salt to penetrate the grain.
Vegetable juices, like the carrot juice used here, make sweet, vibrantly coloured risottos.
We have served this particular variation with salmon and scallop dishes.

SERVES 4

	vegetable oil	
½ cup	onion, diced	125 mL
1 tsp.	garlic, minced	5 mL
2 cups	arborio rice	500 mL
2 tsp.	salt	10 mL
5 cups	carrot juice	1.25 L
2 cups	vegetable stock (page 148)	500 mL
½ cup	white wine	125 mL
½ cup	green onions, sliced	125 mL
1 cup	spinach leaves	250 mL
¼ cup	fresh cilantro, chopped	60 mL
	salt and pepper	

In a heavy-bottomed pot, heat a small amount of vegetable oil. Sauté the onion and garlic until almost transparent. Add the rice and sauté until the grains start to become translucent. Season with the salt.

In another pot, combine the carrot juice and vegetable stock and heat. Set aside and keep warm.

The cooking time for the risotto is 12 to 15 minutes. Add the white wine to the rice and let the rice absorb it. Slowly add the heated stock mixture 1 cup (250 mL) at a time (keep the remaining stock warm). Simmer over medium-low heat, stirring frequently and adding stock as needed; make sure the rice remains just covered with liquid.

Add the green onions, spinach and cilantro. Continue cooking and stirring until the rice reaches a porridgelike consistency. Adjust the seasoning with salt and pepper and serve.

Spinach and basil cannelloni

::

*Michael Allemeier created this when a friend came back from Seattle
with a bag of assertively flavoured Hawaiian basil. The combination of basil and spinach worked well,
and this dish went on the next menu.
It goes nicely with a yellow pepper or tomato coulis.*

SERVES 4

1 lb.	cannelloni sheets	500 g
1 Tbsp.	ollve oil	15 mL
1 cup	onions, diced	250 mL
4	garlic cloves, diced	4
8 cups	spinach leaves	2 L
½ cup	fresh basil leaves	125 mL
1 cup	ricotta cheese	250 mL
2 Tbsp.	Parmesan cheese, grated	60 mL
	salt and pepper	
1 cup	mozzarella cheese, grated	250 mL

Bring a pot of salted water to a boil. Add the cannelloni sheets and simmer for about 8 minutes until tender. Remove and cool in a bowl of iced water. Drain and set aside.

Heat a frying pan and add the olive oil. Sauté the onions and garlic until golden and tender. Place in a bowl and let cool.

Preheat the oven to 325°F (160°C).

Heat another pot of water, then plunge the spinach and basil into it. Remove them right away and cool in a bowl of iced water. When they are cold to the touch, squeeze out the water and chop coarsely.

Add the spinach and basil to the onion mixture. Add the ricotta and Parmesan, then season.

Lay out the cooked cannelloni sheets and fill the bottom third of each with the filling. Roll up the cannelloni.

Place the cannelloni in a roasting pan and cover with the mozzarella cheese. Bake in the oven for 40 to 45 minutes until hot.

Barley risotto
with shiitake mushrooms

::

This recipe can be served as a side dish with roast chicken or fish, or as a hearty vegetarian main dish.
The type of stock used in the risotto can be varied according to the dish it will accompany.
The first time we made this at the restaurant, we used a prawn stock as the base and served it with rare grilled tuna.

SERVES 4

1 cup	pearl barley	250 mL
3-4 cups	stock	750 mL-1 L
2 Tbsp.	butter	30 mL
½ cup	celery, diced	125 mL
½ cup	red onion, diced	125 mL
½ cup	carrot, diced	125 mL
½ cup	fennel bulb, diced	125 mL
1 cup	shiitake mushrooms, sliced	250 mL
¼ cup	dry sherry	60 mL
	salt	
2 Tbsp.	parsley, chopped	30 mL

Rinse the barley to remove any surface starch and drain.

Heat the stock in a saucepan and keep it warm.

In a heavy-bottomed pot, melt the butter and sauté the celery, onion, carrot, fennel and mushrooms until translucent. Add the barley and sherry, stirring to deglaze the pot.

Add enough heated stock to cover the barley (keep the remaining stock warm). Add some salt at this point so that it has a chance to penetrate the grains.

Simmer until the barley is cooked, stirring occasionally and adding stock as necessary to keep the barley covered. This process should take about 30 minutes.

Add the parsley, then season and serve.

Chanterelle and Asiago lasagne

::

As with all of our mushroom recipes, you can substitute oyster, shiitake or
wild mushrooms. If fresh chanterelles are unavailable, we can recommend the canned ones.
This lasagne is good served with a spinach salad.

SERVES 4

2 Tbsp.	olive oil	30 mL
1 lb.	chanterelle mushrooms, sliced	500 g
1 Tbsp.	fresh rosemary, minced	15 mL
1 tsp.	garlic, minced	5 mL
1 Tbsp.	shallot, minced	15 mL
½ cup	white wine	125 mL
1 cup	whipping cream	250 mL
4½ lbs.	spinach	2 kg
1 cup	tomato sauce (page 150)	250 mL
12	cooked lasagne sheets	12
4 oz.	Asiago cheese, grated	120 g
	salt and pepper to taste	

In a frying pan, heat the olive oil and sauté the mushrooms, rosemary, garlic and shallot until tender.

Deglaze the pan with the white wine, then add the whipping cream. Reduce for 15 minutes on medium heat.

Preheat the oven to 350°F (180°C).

Bring a pot of water to the boil and plunge in the spinach. Remove it right away and cool in a bowl of iced water. When it is cold to the touch, squeeze out the water.

Line a 9-inch (23-cm) square baking pan with half of the tomato sauce.

Layer the baking pan in this order: lasagne sheet, mushroom mixture, lasagne sheet, spinach, lasagne sheet, mushroom mixture, lasagne sheet, tomato sauce, Asiago cheese.

Bake the lasagne in the oven for about 30 minutes, until hot and golden brown. Cut into squares to serve.

Pesto linguine
with grilled eggplant and poached bocconcini

::

*In this vegetarian main course, the poached bocconcini melts
into the linguine and becomes part of the sauce.*

SERVES 4

2	medium eggplants	2
1 Tbsp.	salt	15 mL
2	garlic cloves, minced	2
½ cup	olive oil	125 mL
½ cup	shallots, sliced	125 mL
½ cup	white wine	125 mL
2 cups	heavy cream	500 mL
pinch	salt and pepper	pinch
5 cups	vegetable stock (page 148)	1.25 L
14 oz.	linguine	400 g
	vegetable oil	
½ cup	basil pesto (page 151)	125 mL
4	bocconcini	4

Cut the eggplants lengthwise into slices ½ inch (1.2 cm)
thick. Salt the slices and drain on paper towels for 30
minutes. In a bowl, combine the garlic and olive oil, then
add the eggplant and marinate until needed.

To prepare the sauce, combine the shallots and white wine
in a saucepan and reduce by half. Add the heavy cream
and bring to a boil. Season and strain. Reserve until ready
to serve.

Bring a large pot of salted water to a boil. While it is
heating, grill the eggplant slices for 6 to 8 minutes until
tender. Season and keep warm.

In separate pots, heat the sauce and the vegetable stock.
Keep both of them warm.

Add the linguine to the pot of boiling water and cook
until it is al dente. Drain and rinse in cold water. Toss in a
small amount of vegetable oil to prevent sticking.

Whisk the pesto into the sauce and toss the linguine in
the mixture until heated through.

Arrange the eggplant in a ring on the plates, then place
the linguine in the centre.

Using a slotted spoon, lower the bocconcini one at a time
into the simmering vegetable stock for 30 seconds. Place
one bocconcini on top of each plate of linguine. Serve at
once.

Cinnamon basmati rice

::

This is a very traditional Indian way of cooking rice.
Basmati goes well with any of our Indian-influenced
dishes, such as Tandoori Halibut Cheeks (page 76),
Tandoori Chicken Breast with Fruit Chutney (page 99)
or Vegetable Coconut Curry (page 107).

SERVES 4

I cup	white basmati rice	250 mL
1¾ cup	water	450 mL
I tsp.	salt	5 mL
I stick	cinnamon	I stick
3	cloves	3

Wash the rice in cold water to remove the starch and
drain. Put the rice into a heavy-bottomed pot and cover
with the water. Stir in the salt, cinnamon and cloves.

Cover the pot with a lid and bring to a boil, then simmer
for about 15 minutes, until all the water has been
absorbed.

Remove the pot from the heat and let sit for 5 minutes
with the lid still on. Stir to fluff up the rice and serve.

Horseradish griddle cakes

::

Dennis Green recommends using a heavy, cast-iron
frying pan or griddle to cook these.
They require long, steady heat and a minimum of oil.
Starchy potatoes—russet or Yukon gold—are best.

SERVES 4

3 ½ lbs.	potatoes	1.5 kg
2	egg yolks	2
¼ cup	green onions, minced	60 mL
2 Tbsp.	fresh parsley, chopped	30 mL
¼ cup	horseradish	60 mL
	salt and pepper	
	butter	

Preheat the oven to 350°F (180°C).

Wash and prick the potatoes, then bake in the oven for
about 40 minutes until done.

Scoop out the potatoes and discard the skins. Mash using
a potator ricer, a food mill with a coarse blade or a box
grater. Mix in the egg yolks, green onions, parsley and
horseradish. Season.

Form the potato mixture into patties 1 inch (2.5 cm)
thick and 3 inches (7.5 cm) in diameter. Melt a little butter on a griddle or in a cast-iron frying pan and cook over
medium heat, 8 minutes per side, until golden brown.

Mashed potatoes and variations

::

Whoever thought something as humble as the potato could turn into something so sinful?
Unfortunately, the key to great mashed potatoes is cream and butter.
Russets are the best type of potato for mashing.

SERVES 4

MASHED POTATOES

2 lbs.	potatoes, peeled and cut into large pieces	I kg
I cup	heavy cream	250 mL
2 Tbsp.	butter	30 mL
	salt and pepper	

Boil the potatoes in salted water until tender and drain immediately.

Mash the potatoes using a potato ricer or a food mill with a coarse blade.

Scald the cream with the butter and mix into the mashed potatoes.

Using an electric mixer or heavy whisk, whip the potatoes until fluffy. Season.

GARLIC MASHED POTATOES

Crush 3 cloves of garlic and scald with the cream. Allow to steep for 10 minutes to infuse the cream with flavour. Strain before adding to the mashed potatoes.

SUN-DRIED TOMATO AND GREEN ONION MASHED POTATOES

Finely chop ⅓ cup (75 mL) sun-dried tomatoes and scald with the cream. Scalding will soften the dried tomatoes and also give the cream a light pink colour. Just before serving, mix in ¼ cup (60 mL) of finely chopped green onions and 2 tablespoons (30 mL) of finely chopped fresh cilantro. Depending on the salt content of the dried tomatoes, it may not be necessary to add any salt.

>
Wild mushrooms
sautéed with
thyme, pears and
green peppercorns,
page 105

Crisp potato pancakes

::

*These potato pancakes are a good accompaniment to a seafood or meat main dish,
especially the Pan-Seared Scallops with Lemongrass and Chervil Sauce (page 60) or instead of dumplings
with the Shiitake-Stuffed Pork Tenderloin (page 86).*

*Choose potatoes with a high starch content such as russet, Yukon gold or kennebec, as types with a high sugar
content will turn dark and even burn before getting crisp. Also, you want old potatoes, not new.*

*Use an 8-inch (20-cm) frying pan, as pancakes any larger are difficult to turn over without cracking.
If you do use a larger pan, try to limit the size of the cake to a diameter of 8 inches (20 cm),
making sure the edges are even, as ragged edges will burn.*

SERVES 4

½ cup	butter	125 mL
¼ cup	vegetable oil	60 mL
1½ lbs.	potatoes, peeled	750 g
1 tsp.	salt	5 mL
pinch	ground white pepper	pinch

In a saucepan over medium heat, clarify the butter by simmering until all the milk products evaporate and only the butterfat remains. Strain and stir in the vegetable oil.

Shred the potatoes as finely as possible, using a mandoline cutter or grater. Squeeze out as much moisture as possible. Season.

Pour the butter/oil mixture to a depth of ⅛ inch (2 mm) into a cast-iron frying pan over medium-high heat. Add ¼ of the potato mixture and flatten into a thin cake to cover the bottom of the pan. The butter/oil mixture should come halfway up the thickness of the potato; you may need to add a bit more after shaping the cake.

Cook the pancake for 5 to 7 minutes, until the bottom is golden brown and crisp. Turn the pancake over and cook for 5 to 7 more minutes, until the bottom is golden and crisp. Blot on a paper towel.

Any oil left in the pan can be strained and reused to cook the next cake; be sure to remove any little bits of potato that could burn.

Place the cooked pancakes in a single layer on a baking sheet and keep warm in the oven on the lowest setting while you prepare the rest.

<
Warm gingerbread
cake with toffee
sauce, page 136

Nugget potatoes
stuffed with Pernod butter

::

12	nugget potatoes	12
¼ cup	clarified butter **OR** vegetable oil	60 mL

PERNOD BUTTER		
8 oz.	butter, at room temperature	225 g
2 oz.	Pernod	60 mL
2	shallots, finely diced	2

Preheat the oven to 400°F (200°C).

Trim ⅛ inch (2 mm) off each end of the potatoes and stand them up in a roasting pan. Pour the clarified butter (or vegetable oil) over the potatoes and bake in the oven for 40 to 45 minutes until soft. Let cool.

When the potatoes are cool, use the small end of a melon baller to scoop out a bit from each of them.

To make the Pernod butter, whip together the butter, Pernod and shallots in a food processor until smooth.

Pipe the butter into the scooped-out potatoes. Place them on a baking sheet and reheat in the oven at 400°F (200°C) for 10 to 15 minutes.

Desserts

About making desserts

When it comes to baking or making desserts, Michael Allemeier prefers to use metric measures, which are more precise than those given in imperial. To achieve the best results, try using the metric measures. Note that some of these are by weight, which is more dependable and accurate than volume, so watch out for them and use a kitchen scale calibrated in metric.

All-purpose flour will work well in both the cake and pastry recipes. But for even better results with the pastry, use a soft flour.

Death by chocolate

::

This is our restaurant's signature dessert. Lesley Stowe, from whom we bought all our desserts at first, came up with the original recipe and the name; John Bishop turned it into a piece of art by splashing the raspberry coulis over the plate to achieve the colourful "death" effect. Now we put the dessert plate in a box and throw on the coulis from above, but when we prepared a dinner for Pierre Trudeau many years ago (he had two helpings of this dessert), we were still splashing it on without any protection. When the kitchen staff came out to take a bow after dinner, they were covered with red splashes of coulis and looked as if they'd survived a massacre.

MAKES ONE TERRINE (10 TO 12 SERVINGS)

25 oz.	semi-sweet chocolate	700 g
1¼ cups	whipping cream	300 mL
¾ cup	unsalted butter, melted	150 g
6	egg yolks	6
¼ cup	Café Royale liqueur	50 mL
⅔ cup	icing sugar, sifted (optional)	75 g
2 cups	fresh OR frozen raspberries	500 mL

Carefully and slowly melt the chocolate with the whipping cream in a bowl over a hot-water bain-marie, stirring until smooth and free of lumps. Add the melted butter, whisking well to fully incorporate it. Set the chocolate mixture aside, but do not let it cool.

Place the egg yolks, Café Royale and icing sugar in another large bowl over a hot-water bain-marie. Whisk until the mixture is pale, thick and at the ribbon stage. Slowly add the warm chocolate mixture a little at a time to the yolk mixture, whisking well.

Line a 9 × 5 × 3 inch (23 × 13 × 7 cm) terrine or loaf pan with plastic wrap, making sure that the plastic is pushed into all the corners. Pour the batter into the pan and let cool. Refrigerate overnight before cutting.

Purée the raspberries, using a food processor or food mill. Strain the purée through a fine sieve to remove all the seeds. Sweeten to taste with icing sugar if you wish. We use organic raspberries picked at the peak of sweetness, so we don't need to sweeten the coulis.

Use a warm thin knife to cut the chocolate terrine into slices ½ inch (1.2 cm) thick. To serve, place a slice on a plate and splash raspberry coulis over it and the plate to create the "death" effect.

Rhubarb apple crumble
with crème fraîche

::

*Michael Allemeier claims that his mother makes the best rhubarb apple crumble on earth,
but this isn't the recipe for it. He wants to save the experience of eating it for when he visits her.
True to his conviction that he doesn't want to cook exactly what other people, including his mother, are cooking,
he invented this version and serves it with Crème Fraîche (page 53) that has a little cinnamon and sugar
mixed in. Let's just call it the second-best rhubarb apple crumble on earth.*

SERVES 4

CRUMBLE TOPPING

⅓ cup	butter, room temperature	80 g
¼ cup	brown sugar	50 g
2 cups	oats	180 g
⅓ cup	flour	50 g

To make the topping, place the butter and brown sugar in a bowl, then use a wooden spoon to cream them together until smooth. Stir in the oats and fold in the flour, making sure all the ingredients are well mixed.

RHUBARB APPLE FILLING

2 cups	rhubarb, diced	250 g
2 cups	apples, cored, peeled and diced	300 g
1	orange, zest and juice	1
1 tsp.	ginger, peeled and grated	5 mL
½ cup	sugar	125 g
1 Tbsp.	cornstarch	15 mL
1 Tbsp.	water	15 mL

To make the filling, place the rhubarb and apples in a heavy-bottomed pot. Finely chop the orange zest. Add the orange juice, zest, grated ginger and sugar.

Stirring all the time, cook the filling over low heat for 5 to 8 minutes, until the fruit is tender. More liquid will appear as the fruit heats up. Don't let it burn.

In a small bowl, mix together the cornstarch and water.

When the fruit is tender, stir in the cornstarch slurry. Once the liquid thickens, remove the pot from the heat.

Preheat the oven to 350°F (180°C).

You can make 4 individual crumbles or fill one 8-inch (20-cm) square cake pan. Spoon the filling into four ¾ cup (190 mL) ramekins or into the cake pan. Smooth the top and sprinkle on the topping.

Place in the oven and bake for 25 minutes until golden brown.

Raspberry sablé

::

A sablé is a rich, buttery biscuit that is tender enough to be layered with cream and fruit—a French version of raspberry shortcake.

SERVES 4 TO 6

SABLÉ BISCUIT

I cup	unsalted butter, softened	250 g
I cup	icing sugar, sifted	125 g
I	vanilla bean OR	I
2 Tbsp.	vanilla extract	30 mL
½ cup	cornstarch, sifted	75 g
¼ tsp.	salt	2 g
2 cups	flour, sifted	250 g

Preheat the oven to 325°F (160°C).

In a bowl, use a wooden spoon to cream together the butter and icing sugar until smooth and soft. Cut the vanilla bean in half and scrape out the seeds, then add the seeds and husk (or the vanilla extract) to the butter mixture. Add the cornstarch and salt. Mix well.

Add the flour and mix until the ingredients just come together. Do not overmix. Let rest for 30 minutes.

Roll out the dough to a thickness of ⅛ to ¼ inch (3 to 6 mm) and cut out using a round cutter. You will need three rounds for each serving.

Place the rounds on a baking sheet lined with parchment paper and bake in the oven for 10 to 12 minutes. Let cool.

RASPBERRY CREAM

3 cups	fresh raspberries	750 mL
2 cups	whipping cream	500 mL
3 Tbsp.	icing sugar	25 g
	icing sugar for garnish	

Put about 20 per cent of the raspberries in a blender or food processor and purée. Push through a sieve and set aside.

In another bowl, combine the cream and icing sugar, then whip until firm peaks form. Carefully fold the whipped cream into the raspberry purée. Refrigerate until needed.

To assemble, place a sablé biscuit on each plate. Put a dollop of raspberry cream in the centre, then arrange fresh whole raspberries around the cream. Place a second biscuit on top and put a dollop of cream in the centre, then arrange fresh whole berries around the cream. Top with a third bisuit and dust it with icing sugar.

Yam brûlée

::

Although this dish has a flavour much like that of pumpkin pie,
the texture of yams works better than pumpkin in this dish.

SERVES 6

4 cups	water	1 L
¼ cup	sugar	75 g
2 cups	yams, peeled, cut into large, uniformly sized cubes	400 g
2 cups	heavy cream	500 mL
1	vanilla bean OR	1
1 tsp.	vanilla extract	5 mL
⅓ cup	sugar	100 g
9	egg yolks	9
½ tsp.	ground cinnamon	2 mL
½ tsp.	ground ginger	2 mL
	brown sugar to caramelize	
	whipped cream	

Preheat the oven to 325°F (160°C).

Add the water and the ¼ cup (75 g) sugar to a saucepan and bring to a simmer. Add the yams and cook for 15 to 20 minutes until tender. Drain well. Purée the yams until very smooth, using a food processor or potato ricer. Keep warm.

In a stainless steel pot, heat the cream to just under a simmer. Cut the vanilla bean in half and scrape out the seeds, then add the seeds and husk (or the vanilla extract) to the cream.

While the cream is heating, combine the ⅓ cup (100 g) sugar, egg yolks, cinnamon and ginger in a large stainless steel bowl. Whisk until the ingredients are well mixed.

Carefully pour just a few tablespoons of the scalded cream into the yolk mixture to temper it. Then gradually add the rest of the cream, while whisking gently so as not to create any foam on the surface.

Stir in the heated yam purée and incorporate evenly. Strain the custard through a sieve, using the back of a spoon to push through any purée.

Carefully pour the custard into six ¾ cup (190 mL) ramekins. If any bubbles form on top of the custard, pop them using the point of a knife. Place the ramekins in a hot-water bain-marie and bake in the oven for 30 to 40 minutes, until the custard sets. Remove from the oven and let cool.

Once the brûlées are cool, they are ready to be finished. Cover each custard with an evenly spread ¼ inch (6 mm) layer of brown sugar. Caramelize the sugar either by using a blowtorch or by placing the ramekins under the broiler. Let cool and serve with whipped cream.

Vanilla bean ice cream
with orange sugar biscuits

::

We use vanilla beans rather than extract whenever we can for the beautiful, clean flavour.
They are becoming more readily available, so it's easier to get them fresh, which is important.
The seeds are inside the bean, and those tiny black speckles indicate that real vanilla bean has been used in a dish.

MAKES 12 BISCUITS, 4 CUPS (1 L) ICE CREAM

ORANGE SUGAR BISCUITS

I cup	butter, room temperature	225 g
½ cup	sugar	150 g
3 Tbsp.	orange zest, finely chopped	50 mL
I	egg yolk	I
I tsp.	vanilla extract	5 mL
2 cups	flour	275 g
	sugar for topping	

In a bowl, use a wooden spoon to cream together the butter, sugar and orange zest until smooth and not gritty. Mix in the egg yolk and vanilla.

Fold the flour into the butter mixture. Roll out the dough to make a log 1 inch (2.5 cm) thick. Chill in the refrigerator for 1 hour.

Preheat the oven to 325°F (160°C).

Cut the chilled dough into coins about ½ inch (1.2 cm) thick and place on a cookie sheet. Bake in the oven for 10 minutes, then sprinkle with sugar and bake for another 10 minutes. Remove from the oven and let cool.

VANILLA BEAN ICE CREAM

2	vanilla beans	2
2 cups	whipping cream	500 mL
2 cups	light cream	500 mL
8	egg yolks	8
½ cup	sugar	125 g

Cut the vanilla beans in half and scrape out the seeds. Set aside the seeds and the husks.

In a stainless steel pot, slowly bring the whipping cream to a simmer with the husks and seeds of the vanilla beans. Add the light cream and gently bring back to a simmer.

In a bowl, whisk together the yolks and sugar until the mixture is thick, pale and at the ribbon stage.

Temper the yolk mixture by slowly adding the warm cream little by little. Gradually add the rest of the cream while whisking gently.

Return the custard to the pot over low heat, stirring constantly as the custard thickens. It is ready when it will coat the back of a spoon and you can draw a line through it. Strain through a fine sieve and let cool.

Freeze in an ice-cream maker, following the manufacturer's directions.

Serve with the orange sugar biscuits.

Poached fruit with Gewürztraminer syrup
and lemon almond biscotti

::

Use a Gewürztraminer that's not bone dry, because you need a bit of sweetness to carry the fruit.
A number of different fruits work well here—peaches, pears, apricots, figs—all flavours
that turn up in the nose of a good Gewürztraminer.

These biscotti are soft rather than hard, so you don't have to dip them in anything in order to eat them.

SERVES 4

GEWÜRZTRAMINER SYRUP

2	vanilla beans OR	2
2 Tbsp.	vanilla extract	30 mL
	fruit	
1 ½ cups	Gewürztraminer wine	350 mL
4 cups	water	1 L
1 ½ cups	sugar	375 g
2 sticks	cinnamon	2 sticks

Cut the vanilla beans in half and scrape out the seeds. Set aside the husks and seeds.

Use any fresh fruit you wish: one per person for large fruits such as peaches, two or more for smaller fruits such as apricots.

In a stainless steel pot, combine all the ingredients and bring to a simmer for 30 minutes, until the fruit is soft but not mushy.

Remove from the heat and let cool. Steep overnight in the refrigerator.

LEMON ALMOND BISCOTTI

1 ¼ cups	almonds, sliced	150 g
2 cups	flour, sifted	250 g
¾ cup	sugar	200 g
1 tsp.	baking powder	5 mL
¼ tsp.	baking soda	1 mL
¼ tsp.	salt	1 mL
¼ cup	butter, room temperature	75 g
2	whole eggs	2
1	egg yolk	1
1 tsp.	vanilla extract	5 mL
1	zest of lemon, finely chopped	1
	flour	
	butter	

In a food processor, combine the almonds, flour, sugar, baking powder, baking soda, salt and butter. Pulse until evenly mixed and the almonds start to break.

In a bowl, use a fork to beat together the whole eggs, egg yolk, vanilla and zest.

Add the egg mixture to the dry ingredients in the food processor and mix slowly, until the dough just comes together. Remove and knead for 1 minute on a floured

board. Put in a bowl and cover, then let rest in the refrigerator for 1 hour.

Preheat the oven to 350°F (180°C).

Divide the dough into three portions and roll each into a log about 1½ inches (4 cm) thick, using flour if needed to stop the dough from sticking.

Butter and flour a baking sheet, then place the logs on it. Bake in the oven for 15 to 20 minutes. Let cool on the baking sheet for 30 minutes. Cut the logs into slices ½ inch (1.2 cm) thick while still a bit warm and let cool.

Before serving this dessert, strain the poached fruit and reserve the syrup. Serve the poached fruit with some of the syrup poured over it and lemon almond biscotti on the side.

Chilled sabayon
with seasonal berries

::

Forget everything you've heard about having to whip sabayon by hand. Use a hand mixer and save your strength. For this dessert, Madeira is just one of the possibilities—others include an orange-based liqueur, sherry or a late-harvest muscat. Look for whatever berry is in season and buy the freshest ones you can get to ensure the best flavour and quality.

SERVES 4

5	egg yolks	5
I tsp.	vanilla extract	5 mL
½ cup	sugar	125 g
¼ cup	Madeira	60 mL
I cup	whipping cream	250 mL
4 cups	assorted berries	I L

Combine the egg yolks, vanilla, sugar and Madeira in a stainless steel bowl over a hot-water bain-marie and whisk until the mixture starts to thicken. Don't let the water in the bain-marie boil; keep it at a simmer.

Remove the bowl from the bain-marie and whisk the sabayon until it cools to room temperature, then refrigerate until it becomes cold.

In a separate bowl, whip the whipping cream until stiff peaks form, then fold it into the cold sabayon.

Serve the sabayon in bowls with the berries.

Banana tart
with caramel sauce

::

We don't use a lot of adjectives on our menus—we'd rather let the ingredients speak for themselves, as they do in the cooking. But in this case, the name doesn't do justice to the glories of a warm buttery crust filled with rich, sweet bananas in a velvety caramel sauce, with ice cream melting all over it. If that's the sort of thing you enjoy, you'll melt, too.

SERVES 4

CARAMEL SAUCE

1½ cups	sugar	325 g
½ cup	water	125 mL
1½ cups	whipping cream	375 mL

To make the caramel sauce, dissolve the sugar in the water, in a heavy saucepan over low heat. Turn the heat to high and caramelize the sugar until golden.

Remove the saucepan from the heat and carefully add the cream a little at a time, stirring over medium heat until dissolved. Pass through a sieve and let cool.

BANANA TART

1 lb.	all-butter puff pastry	450 g
4	bananas	4
½ cup	sugar	125 g
	caramel sauce	
	vanilla ice cream	

Preheat the oven to 425°F (220°C).

Roll out the puff pastry to a thickness of ¼ inch (5 mm). Cut out 4 rounds that are 6 inches (15 cm) in diameter.

Carefully remove the rounds from the sheet of pastry. Use a fork to prick the entire surface of the rounds.

Peel and slice the bananas. Lay out the slices of one banana around the edge of each pastry round, leaving a ¼ inch (5 mm) border on the outside edge. Sprinkle with the sugar and bake in the oven for 10 to 12 minutes, until the pastry is golden brown and cooked.

Place each pastry round on a plate and pour some caramel sauce over top, then place a scoop of vanilla ice cream in the centre. Serve immediately.

Chocolate brownie pie

::

This isn't sickly sweet, so you can serve decent-sized slices.
Vanilla Bean Ice Cream (page 129) or crème anglaise is the perfect complement.

MAKES ONE PIE

CRUST

¾ cup	flour	75 g
¼ cup	sugar	75 g
2 Tbsp.	cocoa	15 g
¼ tsp.	salt	1 mL
⅔ cup	butter, cubed	150 g
6 Tbsp.	water	90 mL
½ tsp.	vanilla extract	2 mL

FILLING

8 oz.	bittersweet chocolate	225 g
1 cup	butter	225 g
6	eggs	6
1¼ cups	sugar	275 g
2 tsp.	vanilla extract	10 mL
½ tsp.	salt	2 mL
¾ cup	cocoa	100 g
1 tsp.	baking powder	5 mL

To make the crust, place the flour, sugar, cocoa and salt in a food processor. Add the butter and pulse 4 to 6 times until crumbly.

Add the water and vanilla, then pulse until the mixture comes together. Press into a 12-inch (30-cm) flan mould and let rest for 15 minutes.

Preheat the oven to 325°F (160°C).

To make the filling, place the chocolate and butter in a bowl over a hot-water bain-marie and melt together.

In a separate bowl, beat the eggs and sugar together until pale, then add the vanilla. Add the melted chocolate and butter mixture, stirring well.

In another bowl, sift together the salt, cocoa and baking powder. Fold the sifted dry ingredients into the chocolate mixture.

Pour the filling into the pie shell and bake for 35 minutes. Let cool.

Serve with vanilla bean ice cream or crème anglaise.

Nut tart

::

We use a combination of pine nuts, cashews and almonds in our version of this tart,
but you can use any combination of nuts. There's no need to toast them first; they cook in the tart.

MAKES ONE TART

PASTRY

2 cups	flour	250 g
¾ cup	butter, room temperature	160 g
I	egg	I
I tsp.	sugar	5 mL
½ tsp.	salt	2 mL

FILLING

½ cup	butter, room temperature	125 g
I ½ cups	brown sugar	325 g
I tsp.	vanilla extract	5 mL
2 cups	assorted nuts, chopped	300 g
2	egg whites	2

Put the flour on a clean work surface and make a well in it. Cut the butter into small pieces and place in the centre of the well with the egg, sugar and salt. Mix the butter, egg, sugar and salt together in the centre of the well.

Slowly start to draw the flour into the centre of the well, continuing until all the ingredients are mixed together. Knead twice, cover and let rest for several hours before using.

Preheat the oven to 350°F (180°C).

Roll out the pastry and line a 9-inch (23-cm) flan dish.

Half fill the pastry shell with dried beans to weigh down the bottom and keep it flat. Bake in the oven for 8 to 12 minutes until golden. Pour out the dried beans. Let cool.

Preheat the oven to 400°F (200°C).

In a bowl, use a wooden spoon to cream together the butter and brown sugar until smooth. Add the vanilla and nuts.

In another bowl, lightly whip the egg whites until soft peaks form. Fold the egg whites into the nut mixture.

Pour the nut filling into the pastry shell and bake in the oven for 20 minutes. Let cool.

Warm gingerbread cake
with toffee sauce

::

This cake is dense and moist, so it keeps very well. You can refrigerate or freeze it.
To serve, heat the cake for 30 seconds in the microwave and serve warm. Stashed away for emergencies,
it makes a great backup dessert. We serve it with our Vanilla Bean Ice Cream (page 129).

MAKES 3 CAKE RINGS

TOFFEE SAUCE

2⅔ cups	sugar	650 g
I cup	water	250 mL
2 cups	whipping cream	500 mL

To make the toffee sauce, dissolve the sugar in the water, in a heavy saucepan over low heat. Turn the heat to high and caramelize the sugar until golden.

Remove the saucepan from the heat and carefully add the whipping cream a little at a time. Once all the cream is added, stir over medium heat until dissolved. Pass through a sieve and let cool. Serve at room temperature.

GINGERBREAD CAKE

3 cups	water	750 mL
2 cups	molasses	500 mL
I Tbsp.	baking soda	10 g
2 cups	brown sugar	400 g
I cup	unsalted butter, at room temperature	225 g
2	large eggs	2
5 cups	flour	725 g
I tsp.	salt	5 mL
2 Tbsp.	ground ginger	30 mL
I Tbsp.	ground cinnamon	15 mL
2 pinches	ground cloves	2 pinches
2 Tbsp.	baking powder	30 mL

Preheat the oven to 350°F (180°C).

Butter and flour three 7 × 3½ inch (17 × 9 cm) springform or tube pans.

In a saucepan, bring the water to a boil. Remove the pan from the heat and stir in the molasses and baking soda. Let cool until lukewarm.

In a bowl, use a wooden spoon to cream together the brown sugar and butter until smooth. Mix in the eggs one at a time.

In another bowl, sift together the flour, salt, ginger, cinnamon, cloves and baking powder.

Slowly, alternately add the dry ingredients and the molasses mixture to the butter and sugar. Be sure to mix in the sides and bottom. Pass the batter though a sieve to remove any lumps.

Pour the batter into the prepared pans and bake in the oven for 30 to 35 minutes, until a wooden skewer comes out clean. Remove and let cool. While the cakes are still slightly warm, carefully remove them from the pans.

Serve with toffee sauce and vanilla bean ice cream.

Red wine and elderflower sorbet

::

Elderberry trees grow wild here in Vancouver. They're easy to spot in the late summer and fall with their flat sprays of red berries, and in the spring with their cream-coloured clumps of blossoms. The blossoms smell like a New Zealand Sauvignon Blanc and impart an exquisite, unique flavour. If you want to try this anytime but spring, substitute fresh basil. But do try to collect some elderflowers and make the real thing sometime.

MAKES 6 CUPS (1.5 L)

1 cup	elderflowers	250 mL
6 cups	red wine	1.5 L
3 cups	sugar	750 g
3½ cups	water	850 mL
¼ cup	glucose	100 g

Add the elderflowers and red wine to a saucepan over medium heat. Reduce to one-third. Remove from the heat and let steep.

In a heavy stainless steel pot, mix the sugar, water and glucose and bring to a boil, stirring occasionally. Skim off any scum that forms on the surface. Boil for 3 minutes.

Mix the sugar syrup with the red wine and let sit overnight in the refrigerator.

Pass through a sieve. Freeze in an ice-cream maker, following the manufacturer's directions.

Bread

About baking bread

When it comes to baking bread, Michael Allemeier and Dennis Green prefer to use metric measures, which are more precise than those given in imperial. To achieve the best results, try using the metric measures. Note that some of these are by weight, which is more dependable and accurate than volume, so watch out for them and use a kitchen scale calibrated in metric.

All-purpose flour will work well in the bread recipes. But for even better results, use a hard flour.

Focaccia

::

This focaccia recipe is actually a basic recipe for white bread that we use for many items.
It took Michael Allemeier two weeks of close observation to . . . well . . . steal this recipe from a
secretive master pastry chef he worked with in Winnipeg.

Dennis Green finds that the bread always turns out best on Saturdays,
when Michael is making all his sauces and every burner is fired up and the pots are steaming.
Although the cooks get a little overheated, the bread loves it.

MAKES ONE LOAF

2¾ cups	warm water	650 mL
2 Tbsp.	dry yeast	30 g
4 Tbsp.	sugar	50 g
7 cups	flour	1 kg
2 Tbsp.	salt	25 g
¼ cup	olive oil	50 mL
	cornmeal	
	fresh rosemary leaves	

Preheat the oven to 375°F (190°C).

In a bowl, mix together the warm water, yeast and sugar. Let sit until it becomes frothy.

In another bowl, combine the flour and the salt. Stir in the yeast mixture, then mix in the olive oil.

Knead the dough for about 20 minutes to develop the gluten. Place in a bowl and cover. Let rest in a warm place until the dough doubles in volume. Depending on the room temperature, this may take from 40 minutes to 5 hours.

When the dough has doubled in volume, punch it down and let it rise for another 20 minutes.

Roll out the dough to fit a baking sheet 12 × 24 inches (30 × 60 cm). Brush a baking sheet with olive oil and sprinkle it with cornmeal. Place the dough on the baking sheet and let the dough rise until it doubles in volume, then brush it lightly with olive oil and sprinkle the rosemary on it.

Bake in the oven for about 30 minutes, until the bread turns golden brown and sounds hollow when tapped. Remove from the oven and let cool.

Corn and chili bread

::

Cornbread is infinitely variable. You can add finely chopped fresh chilies instead of the red pepper flakes, add bacon or cheese, substitute roasted corn for fresh. You can make it Italian with rosemary and oregano, or Mexican with cilantro. We use up leftover cornbread in the Whole Roast Chicken with Cornbread Stuffing and Chipotle Sauce (page 96) or the Corn and Chanterelle Bread Pudding (page 42).

MAKES ONE LOAF

	butter	
	flour	
I cup	yellow cornmeal	175 g
I½ cups	flour	225 g
½ cup	sugar	125 g
I Tbsp.	baking powder	15 mL
I tsp.	salt	5 mL
I tsp.	red pepper flakes	5 mL
I½ cups	milk	350 mL
2	eggs	2
½ cup	fresh corn kernels	100 g

Preheat the oven to 375°F (190°C).

Butter and flour an 8-inch (20-cm) square cake pan.

In a large bowl, combine all the dry ingredients. In another bowl, combine all the wet ingredients.

Add the wet ingredients to the dry ones and mix together well.

Pour the batter into the prepared cake pan and bake in the oven for 30 to 40 minutes, until a wooden skewer comes out clean. Remove from the oven and let cool.

Wholewheat soda bread

::

Another basic recipe. Because of the brown sugar and the wholewheat flour in it, this bread lends itself better to the addition of spices than herbs. Dennis Green suggests coriander, fennel or poppy seeds, ginger or nuts. He also suggests sprinkling about half a cup of oatmeal on top before putting the bread in the oven.

MAKES TWO LOAVES

	butter	
	flour	
2¼ cups	white flour	300 g
2¼ cups	wholewheat flour	320 g
¼ cup	brown sugar	50 g
1 Tbsp.	baking powder	15 mL
1 tsp.	baking soda	5 mL
1½ tsp.	salt	7 mL
2 cups	buttermilk	500 mL
2	eggs	2
2 Tbsp.	melted butter	30 mL

Preheat the oven to 375°F (190°C).

Butter and flour two 8-inch (20-cm) square cake pans.

In a large bowl, thoroughly combine all the dry ingredients. In another bowl, combine all the wet ingredients.

Add the wet ingredients to the dry and mix them together using a wooden spoon. Do not overmix—just blend the ingredients.

Pour the batter into the prepared cake pans and dust with flour. Bake in the oven for 25 to 35 minutes, until a wooden skewer comes out clean. Remove from the oven and let cool.

Banana maple bread

::

A sweet bread that makes a nice contrast in the breadbasket. This one is also suitable for afternoon tea.

MAKES ONE LOAF

1¼ cups	white flour	175 g
¾ cup	wholewheat flour	100 g
3 Tbsp.	brown sugar	45 mL
2 tsp.	baking powder	10 mL
1 tsp.	salt	5 mL
¾ cup	buttermilk	200 mL
2	eggs	2
¼ cup	maple syrup	75 mL
1 Tbsp.	melted butter	15 mL
2	very ripe bananas, puréed	2

Preheat the oven to 375°F (190°C).

Butter and flour an 8-inch (2-L) square cake pan.

In a large bowl, thoroughly combine all the dry ingredients. In another bowl, thoroughly combine all the wet ingredients.

Add the wet ingredients to the dry and mix them together using a wooden spoon. Do not overmix—just blend the ingredients.

Pour the batter into the prepared cake pan. Bake in the oven for 30 to 40 minutes, until a wooden skewer comes out clean. Remove from the oven and let cool.

Oat crackers

::

*These are similar to Scottish oatcakes
and have a pastrylike texture.
They are a tasty accompaniment to soups.*

MAKES ABOUT 24 CRACKERS

1 ½ cups	Scottish oats	150 g
½ cup	flour	75 g
1 ½ tsp.	salt	7 mL
½ tsp.	baking soda	2 mL
2 Tbsp.	shortening	30 g
6 Tbsp.	cold water	90 mL

In a bowl, mix together all the dry ingredients. Add the shortening and mix. Add the cold water a little at a time, until the mixture comes together as a dough. Cover and let rest for 20 minutes.

Preheat the oven to 400°F (200°C).

On a lightly floured surface, roll out the dough to a thickness of ⅛ inch (3 mm). Cut into triangular shapes.

Place on a baking sheet and bake in the oven for about 10 minutes, but don't let the crackers brown. Remove from the oven and let cool.

Soup Stocks and Other Basics

About stocks

::

You can't make a good sauce without a good stock, and you can't make a good stock without good ingredients and a lot of love. Here are some pointers to keep in mind:

- If possible, use a stainless steel stockpot.
- Start with cold water so the stock does not become cloudy. (Hot water from the tap has been sitting in a hot-water tank, so it's not fresh.)
- Don't skimp on the ingredients. You need them for flavour.
- Simmer, don't boil. Boiling will make the stock cloudy.
- Keep the simmering lively enough so it breaks through the fat on top. If the temperature is too low, the fat will seal off the stock and it might turn sour.
- Use a ladle to remove surface fat while the stock is simmering.
- Remove the scum. It consists of wastes and impurities.
- Allow 3 to 4 hours to make stock (except for fish or vegetable stock, which should take no more than 30 minutes).

The following stock recipes are for large amounts, but you can use the same principles to make smaller quantities. If you buy a cut of meat for dinner and bone it, then roast the bones (not necessary if it's chicken), add some water and a few vegetables, then let them simmer and reduce while you're preparing the meal. Stocks do take time, but they don't require a lot of attention.

Most stocks will keep for 3 to 4 days in the refrigerator and a few weeks in the freezer. It's a good idea to have a selection of frozen stocks on hand. You can also keep bones and meat trimmings frozen until you're ready to make stock.

Chicken stock

::

MAKES 12 CUPS (3 L)

4½ lbs.	chicken backs and necks	2 kg
16 cups	cold water	4 L
3	large carrots, chopped	3
2	leeks, chopped	2
4	celery stalks, chopped	4
2	large onions, chopped	2
1 small bunch	fresh parsley	1 small bunch
5 sprigs	fresh thyme	5 sprigs
2	bay leaves	2
10	black peppercorns	10

Rinse the chicken backs and necks in cold water. Combine all the ingredients in a large stockpot and simmer for 3 to 4 hours while skimming the scum and fat off the top.

Strain the stock through a fine sieve and let cool to room temperature. Refrigerate or freeze.

Fish stock

::

MAKES 14 CUPS (3.5 L)

4½ lbs.	fresh fish bones (white fish only)	2 kg
2	large carrots, thinly sliced	2
2	leeks, thinly sliced	2
6	celery stalks, thinly sliced	6
4	large onions, thinly sliced	4
12 cups	cold water	3 L
2 cups	white wine	500 mL
1 small bunch	fresh parsley	1 small bunch
5 sprigs	fresh thyme	5 sprigs
2 sprigs	fresh tarragon	2 sprigs
2	bay leaves	2
10	black peppercorns	10

Preheat the oven to 450°F (230°C). Place the fish bones in a roasting pan and bake in the oven for about 20 minutes until golden.

Combine all the ingredients in a large stockpot and simmer for 30 minutes.

Strain the stock through a cloth and let cool to room temperature. Refrigerate or freeze.

Shellfish stock

::

Use crab, lobster or prawn shells, separately or in combination. Reserve the meat for use in another dish.

MAKES 8 CUPS (2 L)

8 cups	cold water	2 L
1 cup	white wine	250 mL
2 lbs.	shrimp, prawn, crab or lobster shells	1 kg
2	carrots, thinly sliced	2
3	celery stalks, thinly sliced	3
2	large onions, thinly sliced	2
1	garlic clove	1
1 small bunch	fresh parsley	1 small bunch
6 sprigs	fresh basil	6 sprigs
1 Tbsp.	fresh ginger, peeled and chopped	15 mL

Preheat the oven to 450°F (230°C).

Rinse the shells in cold water. Place them in a roasting pan and bake in the oven (shrimp and prawn shells for 20 minutes, lobster and crab shells for 40 minutes). Crush the shells with a meat hammer or rolling pin.

Combine all the ingredients in a large stockpot and simmer for 30 minutes.

Strain the stock through a cloth and let cool to room temperature. Refrigerate or freeze.

Vegetable stock (nage)

::

2 cups	white onions, diced	500 mL
3 cups	leeks, diced	750 mL
I cup	celery root, peeled and diced	250 mL
I ½ cups	celery, diced	375 mL
I cup	carrots, peeled and diced	250 mL
10	black peppercorns	10
I	bay leaf	I
I sprig	fresh thyme	I sprig
2 cups	fresh parsley	500 mL
6	garlic cloves	6
6	shallots	6
I Tbsp.	sea salt	15 mL
12 cups	cold water	3 L

Place all the ingredients in a stockpot and simmer for 30 minutes.

Strain the stock and let cool to room temperature. Refrigerate or freeze.

Veal demi-glace

::

Ask your butcher to split the veal bones in halves and quarters.
Our veal demi-glace should not be confused with glace de viande, which is reduced to a thick syrup.
Demi-glace is a liquid that will coat the back of a spoon; it has a consistency
somewhere between half-and-half and whipping cream.

MAKES 6 CUPS (1.5 L)

5 lbs.	veal knuckle bones, split	2.25 kg
½ cup	flour	125 mL
4 cups	onions, diced	1 L
4 cups	leeks, diced	1 L
3 cups	carrots, diced	750 mL
2 cups	celery, diced	500 mL
1 tsp.	black peppercorns	5 mL
6 sprigs	fresh thyme	6 sprigs
¾ cup	fresh parsley	180 mL
2	bay leaves	2
⅔ cup	crushed tomatoes	150 mL
16 cups	cold water	4 L

Preheat the oven to 400°F (200°C).

Place the split bones in a roasting pan and bake in the oven for 2 hours until golden brown. Put the bones into a large stockpot, leaving any fat in the roasting pan.

Mix the flour into any fat in the roasting pan. Add the onions, leeks, carrots and celery to the pan and roast in the oven for 20 minutes, until golden brown and tender.

Add the roasted vegetables to the bones in the stockpot, then add the rest of the ingredients. Simmer for 4 hours, frequently skimming off any scum or fat. Strain the stock and remove all the fat from the surface.

Pour the stock into a clean stockpot and reduce by half. Strain and let cool to room temperature, then refrigerate. Keeps for up to 2 weeks. Do not freeze it.

Tomato sauce

::

The tomatoes used in this sauce should be as ripe as possible. If you can put your finger through them, all the better. If you don't have time to make this during tomato season, put the tomatoes in the freezer whole and make the sauce later.

MAKES 6 CUPS (1.5 L)

¼ cup	olive oil	60 mL
4	large onions, peeled and sliced	4
4 cups	canned whole plum tomatoes	1 L
4 cups	canned crushed tomatoes OR	1 L
6 cups	diced fresh tomatoes, cored and seeded	1.5 L

Heat the olive oil in a large stockpot and sweat the sliced onions. When the onions are tender, add the canned whole plum tomatoes. Add the canned crushed tomatoes (or the diced fresh tomatoes). Simmer for 1 hour.

Put the sauce through a food mill and let cool to room temperature. Refrigerate. Keeps for 5 to 6 days. Do not freeze.

Mint sauce

::

Old-fashioned English mint sauce, with its sweet and sour piquancy, is a perfect accompaniment for lamb. The English probably discovered it during the Crusades, because mint and lamb are cornerstones of Middle Eastern cuisine. Many hybrid mints don't have enough flavour, so use spearmint, peppermint or English mint.

MAKES 2½ CUPS (600 mL)

2 cups	fresh mint	500 mL
1 cup	sugar	250 mL
2 cups	vinegar	500 mL

Finely chop the mint and place in a stainless steel bowl.

Combine the sugar and vinegar in a saucepan and bring to a boil.

Pour the hot vinegar mixture over the mint. Let cool to room temperature, then refrigerate.

After 24 hours, strain out the mint out (or just leave it in). Keeps in the refrigerator for 3 to 4 weeks. Do not freeze.

Basil pesto

::

This is one of the handiest things to have around. If you freeze it in small quantities, you can use just what you need. Our recipe makes a very thick pesto, heavy on the basil, nuts and cheese, light on the oil. Use a solid piece of real Parmigiano-Reggiano and grate it yourself—pregrated Parmesan doesn't have any flavour.

MAKES 4 CUPS (1 L)

1 lb.	fresh basil leaves	500 g
5	garlic cloves	5
3 Tbsp.	toasted pine nuts	45 mL
1 Tbsp.	coarse salt	15 mL
1 cup	Parmesan cheese, grated	250 mL
1 cup	extra-virgin olive oil	250 mL

Wash and dry the basil leaves. Put all the ingredients (except the olive oil) in a food processor or blender and grind into a paste.

Put the basil paste into a bowl and gently work in the olive oil until smooth. Refrigerate or freeze.

Mayonnaise

::

Taking the time to bring your eggs (and all your other ingredients) to room temperature will prevent your mayonnaise from separating. Everything emulsifies better at room temperature.

MAKES 2 CUPS (500 mL)

4	egg yolks	4
4 tsp.	Dijon mustard	20 mL
2 Tbsp.	lemon juice	30 mL
2 cups	canola oil	500 mL
1 tsp.	salt	5 mL

Place the egg yolks, Dijon mustard and lemon juice in a bowl or food processor. Mix the ingredients together.

With the food processor motor running, slowly add the canola oil, a few drops at a time, to the yolk mixture. If you add too much oil too fast in the beginning, the mayonnaise will separate.

After adding about a third of the oil, you can start to add the oil a little more quickly. Once all the oil is incorporated, add the salt.

Keeps in the refrigerator for 4 days.

Index